Running Shorts

A Collection of Stories and Advice For Anyone Who Has Ever Laced Up a Pair of Running Shoes

Running Shorts

A Collection of Stories and Advice For Anyone
Who Has Ever Laced Up a Pair of Running Shoes

Joe Muldowney

Copyright © 2011, Joe Muldowney

Cover design by Christina Muldowney

Cover photographs by Rachel Imschweiler

Photographs provided by John Ausherman, Christina Muldowney, Joseph Muldowney, Brian Tonitis.

Editing by: Christina Muldowney, Kelly Muldowney, Jessica Smith.

Cover: Joe Muldowney, Lisa Haas

ISBN 978-1-257-90942-1

May the road rise to meet you.
May the wind always be at your back.
May the sun shine warm upon your face,
and rains fall soft upon your fields.
And until we meet again,
may God hold you in the palm of his hand.

An Irish Blessing

TABLE OF CONTENTS

Warm Up 1

Mile 1–Cut and Run 5

Mile 2–The Starting Line 9

Mile 3–Home 13

Mile 4–Cast of Characters 17

Mile 5–Running Boom 31

Mile 6–Races Boom 35

Mile 7–Running Boom: Part Deux 43

Mile 8–Running Log 47

Mile 9–Seasons 51

Mile 10–OMG! 57

Mile 11–E-I-E-I-O 63

Mile 12–Run 'Til It Hurts 71

Mile 13–Why Do They Hate Us So Much? 79

Mile 14–The Diet Book 85

Mile 15–Excuses, Excuses 91

Mile 16–Frustration . . . Fulfillment 97

Mile 17–Great Races 103

Mile 18–Boston 111

Mile 19–Aging 123

Mile 20–The Best 129

Mile 21–Tales from the Road 135

Finish Line 141
Bibliography 143

WARM UP

For many years I have dreamed of putting on paper the thoughts and experiences I have accumulated over the years thanks to the sport of long distance running. Surely America and the world would possess a burning desire to learn more about this exciting activity from one who has lived it. Then I thought about retirement dinners.

You know those tedious exercises where people who haven't worked with you for thirty years are forced to endure inside stories and jokes that are extremely funny to those who have. You sit there, uncomfortably, as coworkers laugh at what are, to them, hysterically hilarious tales, while you have absolutely no idea what they're laughing at.

Late last summer, as my wife and I lounged on the sandy beach at Isle of Palms, South Carolina, it hit me. My book would be written for the insiders. It would be about runners, and it would be for runners.

So, without the cast of characters, both those included in the chapter of the same name and the many others, named and unnamed, this book would not have been written. Their stories and the events that surround them are the fabric from which this book is woven. We have shared many moments on the road. In the coming pages I will share some of these experiences with you, as you add miles to your running life. Along the way I'll offer tips and advice from my running journey, some of which, I hope, will help with yours.

My children, Kelly, Megan, and Logan have lived with my training and racing for all their lives. They have traveled with me to races, suffered with me when I was injured, and have grown accustomed to my smelly post workout clothing, my crippled gait after a twenty-mile training run or after having competed in a marathon, my elation after a successful race performance, and my depression after a poor one. Their patience and love, through good times and bad, have been immensely important to me.

Christina, my wife, inspired me to write this book. Her suggestions, encouragement, and support, as well as her confidence in my ability to take on this project, enabled me to transpose my thoughts and experiences into words. She is, in every way, the love of my life. She is a remarkable partner.

Finally, this book is dedicated to my father, Joseph F. Muldowney.

Through each trial and tribulation of my life, my dad was always my greatest supporter. I could write an entire book about him. He traveled to my races, sang my praises, and related story after story to fellow spectators, whether or not they cared to hear them.

Once, on a cold, snow-covered day at the Prevention Marathon, near Allentown, Pennsylvania, he embellished the story of how his son, out there braving the nasty weather conditions, was extraordinary, since he was able to complete marathons while suffering from a heart murmur. The crowd around him was probably stunned when I crossed the finish line without the assistance of the paramedics. In my mid-twenties at the time, my father conveniently forgot to inform the folks that I had outgrown my heart murmur when I was three years old.

At a road race in my hometown of Pottsville, Pennsylvania, in which I both directed and participated, my father volunteered to work at one of the water stations, situated about halfway into the race. The temperatures were in the eighties with stifling humidity. My training partner, Gary Comfort, led the race, followed closely by an arch nemesis of ours from the northern part of the state, whom I trailed for third place. As Gary approached, my father jogged next to him, making absolutely certain he received his cup of hydration. Our rival, however, was not so fortunate. Upon meeting my dad at the water station, he desperately grasped for the cup, only to have my father quickly withdraw the all-important nourishment. The runner was perplexed, angry, and empty-handed. A full cup of water reappeared seconds later, as my dad, arm fully extended, placed it into my outstretched hand.

My father loved sports, and immersed himself in any sport in which I participated. He studied rival runners, advised me on which race distances he thought suited me best, and anxiously awaited results from races at which he was unable to attend.

At the 1978 New York City Marathon, a fellow spectator snapped a picture of my dad near Columbus Circle. There he was, squatting down, papers rolled in his right hand, a baseball cap pulled down over his forehead, looking a little like legendary Alabama football coach, Bear Bryant. Perched on the curb, he patiently awaited my arrival. He peered out onto the course, probably using his old Timex watch to determine exactly when I would pass him.

My father died in May of 2007, but he is with me every day. Throughout his life he swelled with pride at my accomplishments, big and small. Making him proud, made me proud.

This book is dedicated to my dad.

I hope I make him proud.

MILE 1–CUT AND RUN

On a glorious autumn day in 1982, my training partner, Brian Tonitis, and I set out from The Stump on an eleven-mile training run.

Brian and I met in 1978, and have logged thousands of training miles together over the years.

Having circled Sharp Mountain, a rocky, wooded expanse south of Pottsville, we began our long descent to a road known as the Gordon Nagle Trail, which leads to the Schuylkill River. We followed the Schuylkill River into the small town of Cressona, home of the aluminum plant, a major area employer. Small, older dwellings dot the narrow, two-lane road. From there, we would follow a path of coal dirt; sandy, black silt that is easy on the joints, but adheres to socks and legs, creating an anthracite shroud on lower extremities. This two-mile path, paralleling a ribbon of railroad track, would take us on the last five miles back to Pottsville.

As we approached the tracks, the whir of sporadic traffic was interrupted by ear piercing heavy metal music blaring from speakers the size of refrigerators. To our right we spotted a group of a dozen or so individuals, clad in torn jeans and leather vests. This rowdy crowd seemed to be enjoying themselves, swilling beer, while harassing both pedestrians as well as any vehicle not to their liking. From the backs of their rusted pickup trucks they took great delight when two skinny figures ambled by in their short shorts and singlets. We were greeted with a barrage of profanity-laced catcalls. Our manhood, mothers, and mode of exercise were called into question.

My temper tends to get the best of me when sufficiently provoked, but my survival instinct told me that this was an occasion when it was best to grin and bear it, so I continued to run, engaging in idle banter with my training partner.

As we stepped onto the railroad track path, about one hundred yards past the party area, I smiled and observed, "I'm glad we didn't piss those guys off."

Brian calmly responded, "Maybe you didn't, but I gave them the finger."

I wasn't astonished, as Brian has been known to have a boxer's grittiness and a salty cockiness about him, so I chuckled as we ambled along, railroad tracks on our left the river to our right. My running mates and I are rarely silent as we run, so our conversation continued.

Suddenly, the ground around us seemed to shake, as if a train were approaching. Without breaking stride, I instinctively turned around. Fear gripped me, and my spine felt like melted ice. Behind us, speeding down the narrow path, dust and smoke billowing in its wake, was not a train, but one of the pickup trucks. It sounded like it had lost its muffler, and was bearing down on us, loaded with several of the partygoers we had encountered a few minutes ago. They were drunk and loud, and ready for a fight. Apparently they had taken offense to the sight of Tonitis' middle finger.

Seconds before being run down, we split, in a fashion of Charleton Heston's portrayal of Moses parting the Red Sea, in *The Ten Commandments*. Adrenaline coursed through my body, and the flight part of my brain kicked in. The truck passed us, and three of its passengers jumped out. A rock buzzed by my head. I did a 180-degree turn and headed toward a steep hill, the gang members in pursuit. Weighed down by beer guts and a prodigious amount of alcohol in their systems, their pursuit faded quickly, as I hurriedly made my way up the hill toward civilization. My heart was pounding so hard, it felt as though it had exploded and was escaping through my ears. Fear gripped me. I literally ran for my life.

My partner was gone. His fate was unknown to me. I skulked and wove my way home, tramping through briar bushes that felt like barbed wire, over a mountain, traversing back roads, avoiding main routes whenever possible. I finally made it to the secluded safe trails of Sharp Mountain, and back to my home, safe and secure.

Hours went by. Finally I received a call from Brian. He was alive and, like me, safely locked behind closed doors

While I opted to take the land escape route, he went by sea. Bloodying himself through his own grove of thick sticker bushes, he made his way to the Schuylkill River, which was never known to be a pristine body of water. Local folklore delights in the fact that during its hundred or so mile journey from northeastern Pennsylvania to Philadelphia, the Schuylkill River carries our local waste downstream to our big-city neighbors.

Brian slogged across the fetid, calf-deep river to the safety of a four-lane highway, where our pursuers wouldn't dare to accost him. From there, he jogged the final four miles home, facing traffic, fearing every pickup truck that came into his sight.

A reminder of his escape appeared several days later, when, undoubtedly brought on by the filthy river water, he acquired a severe foot infection.

When I look back on that day it makes me conclude that Brian's crossing of the river was the symbolic beginning of a triathlon career he still pursues today.

MILE 2–THE STARTING LINE

If you are reading this, you are a runner or are planning to become a runner.

Running is both the easiest and the most difficult sport on earth. Anyone can do it. It is a part of our genetic makeup. Our prehistoric ancestors were often forced to run in order to stay alive. Running is a simple endeavor. One needs only to place one foot in front of the other and attempt to complete a proscribed distance. There are no special skills required. Equipment is minimal.

But just try it.

Running requires an immense amount of dedication. Although it is an ideal way to increase stamina for other sports, only running can make one a better runner. The simple act of putting one foot in front of the other is rarely that simple. One must be prepared to encounter the elements, whether one resides in Miami Beach or in Manitoba. Something called life, with its complex labyrinth of obligations, often vies for the runner's limited amount of training time. And, speaking of time, darkness is the runner's enemy. So are canines, cars, and catcalls.

And then there is the addiction. When you begin this journey, or if you already have, remember, it is addictive. It is a strong, albeit, a positive drug. It is nearly impossible to set a minimal mileage mark and stick with it. An alcoholic cannot survive on one drink. You will want to run more miles. You will crave speed, as you will need to get faster. The guy running ahead of you in the park will become your target. Your time on the course from your house to the cul de sac and back will be slashed. Significant others will wonder why, if you are getting faster, your daily run takes longer. That's simple: you've added an extra mile to your route.

Finally, the most intoxicating, purest, most potent drug offered to the runner will lure you like a moth to a light bulb. You will decide to race. The Polish Sausage 5K, The Smelly Swamp Cross Country Race, The Our Lady of the Unknown Miracle Five-Miler will entice you. These races will jump off the computer screen and beckon you to attend their event. You finish your first race knowing you can run faster next time out. Local competitors will become familiar to you, and soon you will come home and boast, "Well, I finally beat Pete McGuirk today."

From your humble baptism at the 5K (3.1) mile distance, your running appetite will have been whetted, but not sated. You will crave a 10K, a half marathon, and, just maybe, the full 26.2-mile marathon distance.

Whether you begin your running career in high school or in your forties, whether you want to lose weight, or qualify for the Olympic trials, you will run to reach a goal. Every runner in every race is there to achieve an individual mark. It is the purest of sports, and the most democratic. Your social status, race, sex, or ethnicity does not matter when you toe the starting line. When the gun sounds, everyone is equal.

Each year, when hundreds of thousands of Muslims make the Hajj, the holy pilgrimage to the sacred shrine at Mecca, Saudi Arabia, all are required to wear a simple, white robe before entering the shrine. They all look the same, and they all are the same in the eyes of God.

Much like the pilgrims, all runners, at all races, are the same in the eyes of the clock. Oh, and by the way, that clock doesn't lie, so neither can you. In this sport, you can't exaggerate. The competition is between you and the clock. Each race is a race within you. Sure, it's great to win, or to bring home an age group prize, but setting a goal of a certain time, then achieving it, spells victory every time.

Don't worry about getting old. Most runners don't fear age. They embrace it. When runners hit the number nine at the end of their age, it becomes an exciting time, as they prepare to become a "youngster" in the next age group. There they can hope to clean up on the awards in their new age division.

In our sport, we can run in the Boston or New York City marathons, competing alongside the best runners in the world. The average tennis player will not get to play with the Wimbledon champion, and ordinary golfers will never compete in The Masters Championship, but we have the opportunity to run in the same race as the best in the sport.

In our sport, there is not a problem you cannot, literally, run away from. A training run can quell anger, soothe sorrow, and can produce therapeutic effects that Beverly Hills residents would pay the therapist a thousand dollars for.

On your daily run you may solve complex issues, think creatively, figure out how you're going to tell the boss to shove it, ponder the problems of the universe, or simply relax to the sounds of Brad Paisley on your iPod.

When the weatherman tells you it's twelve below zero with a wind chill, he has issued you a challenge. You're going to run in it, you're going to feel it, and then you're gonna tell people about your experience.

When you become a runner, the beach will seem more beautiful. The mountains become more majestic. Home more welcome.

Along the way you are going to develop friendships that will last a lifetime. As you log countless training hours with friends you will embrace their happy moments, and grieve with them during times of sadness. As friends on the run you are profane toward one another at times. You may even have runners' quarrels. Your daily training runs will become like sitting at the bar or going to church. They will be both solemn and vulgar.

You will encounter countless nay sayers along the way. You will be told you look bad. Folks will say, "You need to gain weight," as if that were some calorie-driven badge of honor. Other humorous jibes may include, "You'll freeze your lungs." Medically, this is virtually impossible. "You're gonna soon be crippled." Also, a statistically unproven statement, and, of course, a timeless favorite, "Run, Forrest, Run"

Running is the journey of a lifetime. You have chosen the perfect path to a healthy lifestyle, both in body and mind.

I have continued this journey for more than thirty-five years, and in the coming pages I hope to share my experiences with you.

But this book is not just about me. It is about you and your journey. My experiences as a runner are yours as well. As runners, we may have different ability levels, and we may be from different generations, but we all share common experiences each time we lace up the running shoes.

Lace 'em up now and we'll share some stories.

Joe Muldowney

MILE 3–HOME

My entire life has been lived in what many refer to as the 'Coal Region' of Pennsylvania. Pottsville, Pennsylvania sits on the southern edge of the world's largest vein of anthracite (hard) coal. One hundred years ago coal was king. Today, only 6% of the population of the region is employed in the coal industry.

Pottsville is home to Yuengling, America's oldest brewery. On warm summer days, the sweet smell of the roasted hops permeates the mountain air. Dick Yuengling, the President and sixth generation Yuengling, was my Little League baseball coach when I was twelve years old. In the 1990s, he graciously opened the doors of his Fort Lauderdale condominium to my running partner Randy Haas and me as we ran races in the south Florida area.

A famous author, John O'Hara, was a Pottsville native. He wrote for the local newspaper and lived on Mahantongo Street, a gorgeous, narrow swath of huge, gabled homes formerly owned by the coal barons, who were the equivalent of today's Arab sheiks, when they monopolized the hard coal industry in the late 1800s and early 1900s.

From 1989 to 1997 I had the privilege to serve as mayor of my small city of approximately 15,000, but my story begins on its streets.

Tree-lined Mahantongo Street has been the epicenter of my running world for thirty-five years. Every runner has a Mahantongo Street. It may be a specific thoroughfare, a park, or a trail, but we all have a running area that defines us.

Since my return from college I have resided near the western end of Mahantongo Street. I have reaped the benefits and felt the pain of the one and one-half mile, narrow, pitched incline. It begins at Centre Street, where Pottsville's once vibrant downtown throbbed with activity. Rounding the corner to begin the climb, one passes the former Necho Allen hotel. In 1790, Necho Allen discovered the flammable black rocks that fueled the economy during the early days of Pottsville. A quarter mile later the Yuengling Brewery sits on the left, conjoined on its eastern edge to Saint Patrick's Roman Catholic Church. This lower end of Mahantongo Street is a steep half-mile incline that levels slightly past the spacious Victorian mansions of the next few city blocks. Twenty blocks west of Centre Street has been the terminating point for thousands of workouts: The Stump.

The overgrown site of a former 50-foot oak tree, The Stump no longer exists as a real entity, rather as a mythical icon to workouts gone by. Sounds at The Stump are the same as sounds at anyone's workout terminus: The high-pitched beep of a watch, a sigh of relief, a 'whew,' or an expletive at the end of a run. A short walk up the hill to my home ends most training runs.

Mahantongo Street, however, goes on. The paved road flattens out past a cemetery and a Little League baseball field, ending a mile later at the Pottsville Club, an exclusive dinner club and the site of a former ski lodge.

A 300-foot elevation rise peaks at the summit of Sharp Mountain, a labyrinth of secluded trails resting on a mountain of coal. From here, one has a majestic view of the city of Pottsville. On a given workout, deer, turkey, and even an occasional black bear may be encountered in the mountain. All Sharp Mountain paths lead back to civilization, and to the undulating roads of the county that challenge us on our daily workouts.

In my region and in places all over the country, the fitness boom has generated funding for the construction of trails, some transformed from old, abandoned railroad beds. The Schuylkill River Trail is one such endeavor, and it has produced magnificent results. Covering a distance of approximately 130 miles, when completed, the trail begins in the City of Philadelphia and follows the Schuylkill River, terminating, for now, in the tiny town of Auburn, in Schuylkill County. Pronounced "skookill," the river was given its name in the 1600s, by Dutch traders. Since the waterway was largely obscured by trees, the Dutch word, "Schuylkill," means, "Hidden."

The trail is flat, scenic, and beautiful. The portion in my backyard covers six miles from Hamburg, at the foot of the Blue Mountain, to Auburn. Runners, hikers, cyclists, and horseback riders utilize the trail.

Wherever you live in America, you have the opportunity to utilize many running venues. Take advantage of them all. Go urban and run in the city. Enjoy the scenic trails. Become faster by running your speed workouts on the local track. If you are near a beach or mountains, appreciate the majesty of both.

Most days on the roads and trails will be relaxed and peaceful. During some workouts, however, you will be the aggressor; while during others, you will be the hunted, as most runners are as competitive as you.

We live in a big country, on a big planet. On your daily training runs, experience as much of it as you can, by not only observing the wonder around you, but by being a part of it.

You'll have many stories to tell.

MILE 4–CAST OF CHARACTERS

Predecessors of the Romans, the Etruscans invented the arch. Some two thousand eight hundred years ago, this architectural innovation featured carved stones, in a semicircular pattern, held together in the middle, by a keystone. Throughout my thirty-five years of running I have been fortunate to have running partners that have become my keystones. Like the Roman stone structure, they have held my running career together.

I have never enjoyed the "loneliness of the long distance runner." Running, for me, has always been a social as well as an athletic activity. Over the years, many runners, playing supporting roles, have come and gone, but a stellar cast of characters has remained, continuing to train and continuing to succeed, through sheer hard work and commitment. They have earned my admiration and respect. They have become my closest, most loyal friends, and we all have enjoyed good times while enduring life's difficult challenges together. Throughout this book you will read about some of their exploits.

Here are the cast members, in alphabetical order.

Eric Anchorstar – Pottsville, Pennsylvania -- Eric is short in stature, but long in dedication. A former weightlifter, Eric sports a pair of biceps the size of softballs, not typical for most spaghetti-armed runners. Shirtless on any day the temperature tops sixty degrees, his sculpted torso contrasts our sunken chests. With his shaved head and several tattoos adorning his arms and chest, he is an imposing figure on the roads. Eric still lifts weights on a regular basis, consistently bench pressing more than 300 pounds. His ink memorializes his three Boston Marathon appearances. In 2004, he turned in a personal best 2:59:18 at the Philadelphia Marathon. At age forty-three he trains hard every day, and manages to maintain the physique of a bodybuilder while running commendable race times.

18   *Running Shorts*

His running regimen consists of about 40 to 50 miles a week, including a speed workout on the track and a long run on weekends. He is the enforcer of our group, who refuses to yield to unruly youngsters, irate motorists, and canines.

John Ausherman – Chambersburg, Pennsylvania -- The relationship between John and me is a classic scenario that exists in all sports, at all levels: athletes who fiercely compete against one another, respecting each other's abilities, yet hoping to beat the snot out of the other guy once the competition begins. Throughout the 1980s John and I battled in many epic running duels at races up and down the east coast. At the 1983 Philadelphia Distance Run, John and I traded leads throughout the 13.1-mile race. He crossed the finish line in a time of 1:08:06; while I clocked a 1:08:08. Our rivalry took us to Washington, D.C., where, at the 1983 Cherry Blossom Ten-Miler, he nipped me again, running 51:40 to my 51:41. At the Boston Marathon, my fastest marathon time of 2:22:54 in 1983 eclipsed his best of 2:24:33 in 1984. In 1986 we duked it out again in Philadelphia. This time I crossed the finish line in a 1:08:54 while John smoked his fastest half marathon time, clocking a 1:07:53. At the 1988 Cherry Blossom, our rivalry continued. My time of 52:53 bested his effort by only ten seconds, as he ran 53:03. And at Boston of that year, I turned in a 2:27:41 to his 2:28:19.

Such was our rivalry, punctuated only with grudging smiles and weak congratulations. Our conversations were usually respectful but brief. Privately, we referred to each other as "that Ausherman guy," or "that Muldowney." Ironically, on a hot July day in 1992, on a family vacation in Myrtle Beach, South Carolina, I ran into John on a boardwalk at a popular tourist destination called Barefoot Landing. We exchanged pleasantries and discovered that we were renting condos a quarter mile away from each other on the beach. For the rest of the week we met early each morning for our daily workout. During our runs on the beach and on the roads I found my rival to be one of the most gracious individuals I had ever met. We trained intensely, and he invited me to come to his home and participate in a memorial race he had established in honor of his father, Tom Ausherman, an ex-Marine, and trailblazer of distance running in southern Pennsylvania, who had passed away after having completed a two-mile race in Hagerstown, Maryland in 1987.

I took John up on his offer, attended his race, and was afforded the hospitality, not only of his family, but also by many of John's friends and members of the Chambersburg community. What began as an intense rivalry has developed into a lifelong friendship. Throughout the years we have raced and socialized together. John introduced my son, Logan, and me to deer hunting. We both shot our first deer on his magnificent spread of land in south central Pennsylvania, and have continued to make deer season at the Ausherman camp an annual tradition. My son, now a United States Marine, possesses a great respect for John, and the two of them correspond frequently. I was honored to share in his daughter, Lindsay's, wedding. As opposed to the seconds that separated us in many of our races, one hundred miles separate us today. I attend his race annually, and our families get together often, thanks to this valuable friendship, borne on the roads.

Gary Comfort – Pottsville, Pennsylvania -- Gary is a distance running pioneer. He was my first running mentor. When I returned home after college in 1975, Gary introduced me to road racing and within a year I was hooked. Comfort is a six-foot two, two-by-four. He may possess the most perfect running form I've ever seen. Gary was an excellent high school runner, and after a brief hiatus, went on to run for Millersville University, located in south central Pennsylvania. During the mid to late 1970s he was unbeatable. His massive, lanky strides gobbled up yards of real estate with each footfall.

Whether he is running fast or slow, he appears to glide, feet barely touching the earth. Gary was the street-corner dealer who started me on my running addiction, and for that, I owe him a huge debt of gratitude.

Gary Comfort(left) next to Joe Muldowney, Prevention Marathon Allentown 1978

In 1981 Gary turned in a stellar performance at the Boston Marathon, covering the course in two hours, 23 minutes. Over the years, knee injuries have curtailed his racing career, although he still runs several times a week. At age fifty-eight, he no longer enters races, but, if he returned to training in earnest, he could still be a formidable running force.

Rob Crosswell – Pottsville, Pennsylvania -- From 1985 to 1998 I owned an athletic footwear business in Pottsville called Marathon Sports. One sunny spring day in 1985, a customer entered my store inquiring about a new pair of running shoes. The gentleman, in his late thirties, appeared to be an ex-wrestler, with a thick frame, wide legs, and a waist that had suffered a few years of expansion. His short frame exhibited explosive power, and his will to succeed in the sport was evident from our first encounter at which he informed me that he was training seven to nine miles daily on a busy road near our homes. He knew little about distance running, but was eager to learn. Coaches often talk about athletes who they feel are "coachable." During Rob's distance running days, he was the most coachable person on the planet.

Standing at around five feet, nine inches tall, and possessing a deep love for food and beverages, Rob felt a need to work harder than his running competitors in order to both keep his weight in check and to defeat them. Most of his local rivals *looked* a lot better than Rob, as they were svelte and trim, but Rob's fanatical work ethic overshadowed their distance running physiques. In any endeavor, he hated to lose. Consequently, in the mid to late 1980s, he would consistently run seventy to one hundred miles a week, always at a pace that averaged below seven minutes a mile. His hard work paid big dividends when, in 1987, at the age of thirty-nine, he ran a time of two hours 49 minutes for the Boston Marathon. For a guy who sometimes struggled to keep his weight under two hundred pounds, that achievement was epic. Upon hearing the news of Rob's marathon, Brian Tonitis observed, "That's amazing! Imagine that. A guy with absolutely no running talent turning in that kind of time." His words were more a testimony to Rob's dogged work ethic rather than a criticism of his physical ability.

Not long after his marathon success, Rob began to experience excruciating knee pain brought about by the fact that, in his right knee, cartilage had eroded to the point that bone was rubbing bone. The compression caused by each foot strike made it impossible for him to continue running, so he embarked on a new athletic endeavor. Rob Crosswell became a skater.

I'm talking about a skater on roller blades traversing the narrow, hilly, pothole riddled streets of our hometown. A skater who, for the past fifteen years has met me for our daily runs of anywhere from four to twenty miles. A skater who incurs the wrath of drivers, who skates in sub-zero temperatures, and sometimes through icy patches and around snow banks. A skater who has dislocated bones and suffered concussions, and who has displayed more strawberries on his bare-chested upper body as a result of encounters with the street than most of our local produce growers.

Now in his early sixties, Rob Crosswell continues to skate sixty to seventy miles a week. He pirouettes through the streets, does speed workouts where he produces speeds of twenty-five miles per hour, and zigzags down hills that would cause mountain goats to question their sanity.

Rob Crosswell

Ryan Crosswell – Miramar, California -- Ryan, thirty, is the son of the aforementioned Rob Crosswell, and he shares many of his father's obsessive-compulsive training tendencies. Entering his senior year in high school, Ryan decided he was going to become a distance runner. Having wrestled he was in good physical condition, so during the summer prior to his senior year he began to routinely run seven miles a day. His efforts enabled him to turn in a stellar cross country season and to run the 3200-meters (two miles) in a time of 10:07. Upon graduation he attended Vanderbilt University, where he earned a spot on the cross country team as a walk-on. A series of injuries, however, cut short his collegiate running career.

Ryan Crosswell attended Duke University Law School, from which he earned his degree. Prior to his graduation, he decided, in his words, that "he wanted to serve," so he joined the United States Marine Corps as an officer training candidate. His dedication to running and fitness enabled him to score among the top of his class in his physical fitness tests, where he routinely ran three-mile timed runs in less than sixteen minutes.

Today Ryan Crosswell serves his country as a Marine Corps Captain.

From his senior year in high school, throughout his college years, and during his time in the Marines, Ryan has continued to remain true to his running roots. Despite a cycle of injuries, he has run a 2:45 marathon, and trains with his father and our running community whenever he returns home.

Mike (Iron Mike) DiCello – Pottsville, Pennsylvania - Standing at about six feet, two inches tall, Mike looks a little more like an outside linebacker rather than a runner, but his perseverance enabled his marathon time to plummet to near three hours in his younger days. At age forty-nine, he has battled a series of knee injuries, but continues to train on a limited basis. Mike doesn't run. He lumbers. His large legs move with power not speed. Each step appears to involve a great deal of labor on his part.

Iron Mike is a confirmed bachelor, fiercely independent, and somewhat of a loner. He is completely inflexible when it comes to scheduling. Family vacations at the Jersey Shore sometimes revolve around Mike's training and recovery schedule, a trait that can cause a great deal of frustration to both family members and training partners.

Mike has a unique job. He works at a local sewage treatment plant.

Frequently, during training runs, the cast would take great delight in quizzing Mike about the details of his work day. For years we threatened to design a racing singlet for him that would feature the name of his employer, followed by a string of turds.

During a track workout, as Lisa Haas, Dicello, and I circled the oval Lisa commented that someone smelled good. Mike replied, "It can't be me. I just spent my day working in a shit plant."

Despite his rather obsessive-compulsive nature Mike remained an integral member of the cast for many years, sharing the joys and disappointments we all experience in our worlds of running and racing.

Lisa Haas – Orwigsburg, Pennsylvania -- At age forty-three, Lisa has distinguished herself as one of the top women's Master's runners on the east coast. She began her career as an excellent track and cross country runner at North Schuylkill High School, and has continued to excel. Her diminutive stature, barely reaching five feet and weighing around ninety-eight pounds, belies a giant drive that is illustrated by vicious training runs and gut busting speed workouts on the track. Lisa's short legs produce massive strides that chew up earth and grind opponents into the ground. We began training together around twenty years ago, and continue to this day. Lisa's extraordinary times include a personal best of 16:40 for the 5K and 28:20 for the five-mile distance. At the 10K distance she has posted a 34:32, and a 1:17:52 for the half marathon. Her marathon best is an amazing 2:46:05, turned in at the age of 40. In 1996 both she and her husband, Randy, qualified for, and participated in the United States Olympic Trials in the marathon. She has also won the prestigious Berwick Run for the Diamonds race.

26   *Running Shorts*

Randy Haas – Orwigsburg, Pennsylvania -- Randy appeared at Marathon Sports one day back in 1986. After a stellar high school running career he had decided to revive his training after having adopted a sedentary lifestyle. We have been running together ever since. Our races have taken us up and down the east coast from Massachusetts to Florida. Blessed with extraordinary talent, he compliments his gift with hard work. At age forty-nine he is still winning races and running well. His achievements and exploits will be chronicled in a later chapter.

Randy Haas (left)
Fort Lauderdale, Florida 1987

Brian Tonitis – Auburn, Pennsylvania -- Since the late 1970s, Brian and I have been both good friends as well as training partners. We have gone through personal triumphs and failures, and have remained friends and confidantes throughout. We have watched our kids grow up and witnessed our parents grow old, both of us having lost, at this writing, one parent. Thirty years ago we consistently logged more one hundred mile weeks together, as we supplemented a minimum amount of talent with a great deal of hard work. Brian turned in two 2:39 marathons at his running peak. Suffering from chronic hamstring problems, his running career veered into triathlons and cycling events, at which he excelled.

Two summers ago Brian ran a tremendous triathlon in Hazleton, Pennsylvania, placing fourth overall and winning the fifty and over age division. Basking in the glow we all experience after a successful race, his joy rapidly vanished, as he experienced profuse sweating and a tight stabbing pain in his chest. His wife, Sue, a medical professional, summoned the emergency personnel. The verdict was clear: my friend of more than thirty years, a man who trains ten to fifteen hours a week and has the heart of a horse, had suffered a heart attack. He was flown by helicopter to Lehigh Valley Medical Center in Allentown, where doctors discovered a 90% blockage of an artery. It seems as though, having completed a race, with trained medical folks nearby, had gone a long way in saving Brian's life. His heart attack was serious, and a sedentary individual may not have fared so well, but Brian was too physically fit and too driven to let this serious threat to his life get him down. Today, two years later, outfitted with a stent to keep his artery open, he is, once again, running, cycling, and swimming. With a new lease on life, he is competing and doing well. Always a bit irreverent, Brian boasts an unfair advantage now that he possesses a refurbished artery and increased blood flow. Of course, the cast of characters, forever unforgiving, informs him that, although he's been a friend for many years, don't expect to receive mouth-to-mouth resuscitation from us any time soon if he decides check out on us during a training run!

Brian Tonitis(right)
Hess's 10K 1979

Matt Tonitis – Auburn, Pennsylvania -- He is Brian's oldest son. I've known Matt, literally, since he was born. He ran cross country and track at Pottsville Area High School, and then became my top runner when I coached him at our local Penn State campus. For the past three years he has become a member of the cast, and his distance running career is in its infancy. He has already run a 2:59 marathon, and will get much better. Following in his father's shoes, he also participates in cycling and triathlon races. Matt is a dedicated trainer and meshes seamlessly with the cast of characters. He has become our historian, having researched our races and times from the glory days, as well as having absorbed the stories acquired from his dad.

30   *Running Shorts*

Matt Tonitis
(right)
Philadelphia
Marathon 2010

Every runner has their own supporting cast. I have been fortunate enough to have had a core group of individuals from whom I have learned, and with whom I have shared a multitude of running experience and lore.

Start your watches as we share some of our adventures with you in the coming pages.

MILE 5–RUNNING BOOM

Few Americans knew what a marathon was on September 9, 1972.

In fact, distance runners were a rare and strange breed, whose ilk confined themselves to secluded ovals where they grinded out lap after lap, and raced at confusing distances that seemed to oscillate between English and Metric measurements.

On September 10, 1972, however, everything changed.

Americans had taken a great interest in the 1972 Summer Olympic Games in Munich, Germany for a variety of reasons.

Four days earlier the world was stunned when a grainy television feed depicted the horror of hooded terrorists holding members of the Israeli Olympic team hostage. Their demands, a bungled rescue attempt, and the death of eleven Israeli athletes, as well as their captors, and a Munich police officer, cast a morbid shadow over the games that were supposed to foster goodwill among nations.

Earlier in the games, American, Mark Spitz, electrified the swimming world by capturing six gold medals.

After having won sixty-two consecutive games in the Olympics, the U.S. men's basketball team lost the gold medal to the Soviet Union, in what may have been the most controversial finish to a basketball game in Olympic history.

Then, on September 10, as the Games prepared to close, many Americans watched this strange event called a marathon. It was 26.2 miles and it was run through the streets of the city. Most Americans wondered how and why such an odd distance race found its way into the Olympics.

In 490 B.C. the Greeks pulled off an upset victory over a much stronger Persian army, on the Plain of Marathon, some twenty-five miles from Athens. According to legend, a Greek messenger named Pheidippides, ran back to Athens to proclaim the triumph. He shouted, 'Nike,' the Greek word for victory, and then he dropped dead.

In 1896, at the inaugural modern Olympic Games in Athens, the long-distance race, symbolizing the glory days of ancient Greece, was revived. Its length was approximately the same as the distance traveled by the ill-fated Pheidippides.

At the 1908 Olympic games in London, the Queen Alexandra requested that the marathon race begin near the back lawn of Windsor Castle, with the finish at London's Olympic stadium. The distance turned out to be 26 miles, 385 yards.

Coincidentally, America's only success in the Olympic marathon occurred in 1908. Italian Dorando Pietri entered the Olympic Stadium in first place, with a comfortable lead. As he neared the finish line his legs turned to jelly and he collapsed onto the dirt track, a victim of exhaustion. Well-intentioned race officials assisted him across the finish line, but this "illegal assistance" led to his disqualification, and second-place finisher, American Johnny Hayes, was awarded the gold medal.

At the 1972 Olympic Games, Frank Shorter, a twenty four year old Yale graduate who was pursuing a law degree at the University of Florida, entered the marathon as a pre-race favorite. Experts believed he could end America's sixty-four year Olympic drought in the long-distance event.

By the halfway point in the race, Shorter, who looked like a vertical hyphen, with a straight-up style of running and a bushy black mustache, had built up a formidable margin over the second-place runner. As he ambled comfortably into the Olympic stadium, however, he was shocked at the sight of another runner in the lead, nearing the finish line. A fitting symbol of a bungled Olympic Games, an imposter had pulled a prank by running onto the course, outside of the stadium. For a time, spectators in the stadium believed he was the pending winner. Officials finally unceremoniously yanked him from the track. American Frank Shorter had won the Olympic Marathon, and America's "Running Boom" had begun.

Four years before Frank Shorter's remarkable feat in Munich, Dr. Kenneth Cooper, a former Air Force Colonel, wrote a best-selling book entitled, *Aerobics*, in which he reported his extensive research on the impact of exercise on health.

Dr. Cooper outlined an 'aerobic,' exercise regimen of 20 minutes a day that represented a minimal level of fitness. This fitness level could be achieved by running, walking, swimming, or cycling. His definition of aerobic exercise was a sustained level of a high heart rate for a prolonged amount of time.

Millions of readers adopted Cooper's philosophy, and Shorter's high-profile Olympic triumph endorsed long distance running as a means of achieving aerobic fitness.

Meanwhile, out in the Pacific Northwest, a coaching legend at the University of Oregon, Bill Bowermen, injected his spark into America's running boom. In 1962, Bowerman took a trip to New Zealand to meet with the respected New Zealand distance running coach, Arthur Lydiard. Lydiard's advice allowed Bowerman to take his track and field coaching abilities to a new level. Lydiard introduced Bowerman to the concept of jogging for fitness. Upon his return to the states, Bowerman not only published a book, called, *Jogging*, in 1966, but started a running club from his home in Eugene. Soon, folks of all ages showed up at the University of Oregon track for Bowerman's 'jogs,' which brought fitness into the adult mind sets of Americans.

With nothing more than a handshake, Bill Bowerman formed a business partnership with one of his former University of Oregon milers, Phil Knight. Together, they began a running shoe distribution company. Knight managed the business affairs while the coach worked on the design of the shoes. After destroying his wife's waffle iron, Bowerman invented the waffle sole design. Their company, originally called Blue Ribbon Sports, soon exploded into Nike, Incorporated.

Dr. Kenneth Cooper provided the theory and research, Coach Bill Bowerman formed the theory into practice; Frank Shorter gave the movement worldwide publicity. This triumvirate ignited the running boom of the 1970s.

It seemed as though everyone was running, and soon races would spring up everywhere.

34   Running Shorts

Gary Comfort top left, Joe Muldowney top third from left

PA. STATE CHAMPIONS
24 HOUR RELAY - JULY 31, 1977
267 MILES, 1,364 YARDS

MILE 6–RACES BOOM

The running boom was launched in the early 1970s. By the mid '70s, it had gone into orbit.

Running, an activity that had been kept in the closet for many years, had a 'coming out' party in the mid '70s. Footraces became fashionable. Everyone wanted to run in a race, and everyone, it seemed, tried to conduct a race. Churches, fire companies, hospitals, tourist attractions, automobile dealerships, and festivals all wanted to add a running race to their list of activities.

Races were relatively small, but numerous. One hundred runners or more generally attended these local events. If you were there, you remember these races. If you weren't, try to picture a group of long-haired runners, mostly male, showing up for a race in colorful, nylon jogging suits, short, snug running shorts, and high, white socks. Most of these races have gone the way of bean bag chairs, pet rocks, and banana seat bikes, but a look back on them is both nostalgic and amusing. So, I'll don my bright green, nylon jogging suit slip on my Nike Mariahs (not the singer the shoes) and we'll take a look at some of the interesting races I participated in during the 1970s and 1980s.

In May of 1976 I entered my first road race. Of all the tiny hamlets in America, my first foray into road racing occurred in one of the most picturesque and interesting places.

Jim Thorpe, Pennsylvania, is a small community of around 4,000 residents that serves as a gateway into the Pocono Mountains. Its Alpine beauty has earned the town the moniker, "Switzerland of America." Josiah White founded the town in 1818, naming it Mauch Chunk, meaning "bear mountain" in the Native American Lenni Lenape language. Apparently the name referred to a local mountain that resembled a sleeping bear.

In 1876, Mauch Chunk was the site of one of the famous trials of the Molly Maguires, a secret society of Irish coal miners, four of whom were accused of kidnapping and murder, subsequently, and in a controversial manner, convicted, and hung on the gallows on scaffolding erected behind the Carbon County Courthouse in Mauch Chunk.

Like many small American towns, Mauch Chunk became more obscure as the 20th century wore on. A mass exodus of population and jobs left the area, or in this case, areas, of East and West Mauch Chunk, forcing the towns to grasp for anything to revitalize the economy of the region.

Then along came Jim Thorpe.

Jim Thorpe, an American Indian who grew up in Oklahoma, spent much of his youth at the Carlisle Indian School, located in south central Pennsylvania. In 1907, it is alleged that he walked past a group of athletes practicing the high jump. While still clad in street clothes, he launched an impromptu jump of five feet, nine inches. Thorpe became a tremendous track and field athlete, but his athletic abilities extended to baseball, football, lacrosse, and even ballroom dancing.

In 1912, The Carlisle Indian School, led by Jim Thorpe, won the national collegiate football championship, but it was in Stockholm, Sweden, at the 1912 Olympic Games where the Jim Thorpe legend would be born. At the Games, Thorpe won the Pentathlon, a sport consisting of five events, as well as the Decathlon, a ten-event competition causing King Gustav of Sweden to proclaim, "You, sir, are the greatest athlete in the world."

Prior to Thorpe's Olympic participation, he accepted meager compensation for playing baseball during his summer vacations. Strict Olympic rules forbid the acceptance of any type of the remuneration; thus, Jim Thorpe was stripped of his Olympic medals.

When he died in 1953, his widow became angry because the state of Oklahoma refused to erect a monument for her late husband.

Far from Oklahoma, Mauch Chunk's town fathers came up with an idea. In an effort to bolster tourism in their town, why not obtain the dead Olympian's remains, unify and rename East and West Mauch Chunk in honor of the Olympic champion? Thorpe had never even set foot within 100 miles of Mauch Chunk, but Thorpe's wife thought it was a great idea, so she obtained her memorial and the town had its tourist attraction. She sold his remains to the town, and a monument was promptly built there in his honor, at the site of his new grave.

In 2010, Thorpe's son sued the town, hoping to have his father's remains returned to Oklahoma.

Today, the quaint town of Jim Thorpe conducts several footraces, a triathlon, and a terrific St. Patrick's Day celebration, but my initiation to road racing was a quadriceps nightmare. The Jim Thorpe 10K began at the top of Flagstaff Mountain, outside of the town, proceeded down a steep hill, through the historic downtown for another two miles, then proceeded back up the other side of the bowl, past the dead Olympian's grave, to a finish at the local high school stadium. By the end of the 6.2-mile event, the longest distance I'd ever raced, I felt as though, like the convicted members of the Molly Maguires, I was dangling at the end of a rope...with very sore legs, feeling as though I belonged in the grave next to the dead Olympian.

1976 was America's Bicentennial. Two hundred years earlier, down the road in Philadelphia, fifty-six brave men penned their names to the Declaration of Independence. From sea to shining sea America celebrated with parades, parties, and, of course, road races.

7.6 in '76 was a popular race distance. Yes, there were many 7.6 mile events, such as the one held in Hamburg, Pennsylvania, a small town north of Reading. 180 runners participated in that and many other Bicentennial races that were, at least, close to the odd 7.6 mile distance.

One such 'attempt' to nail the 7.6 mile distance occurred at a race in the small village of Waverly, New York, located just across the Pennsylvania border.

Gary Comfort and I decided to make the three-hour journey to participate in this race, which was contested on the rural roads and trails of the area. The race went well, for us, and as we awaited the awards ceremony, the post race camaraderie was interrupted by angry shouts, which were greatly amplified by the quiet wooded setting.

"Give us our f*&%ing trophies. Where are our f&*%ing trophies?"

Two young men, clearly upset upon having made wrong turns on the curiously marked course, vehemently vocalized their concerns to the over two hundred runners and race officials gathered for the awards presentation. It still ranks as one of the most amusing race protests I've witnessed. Despite the unplanned post-race entertainment, the runners did not receive their f*&%ing trophies.

Another 7.6 for '76 race was held at the Daniel Boone Homestead, between Reading and Pottstown. Daniel Boone, the famous frontiersman, although usually associated with Kentucky, spent his youth there. His homestead is located in a quiet, wooded valley, and the race was contested in the fields of high grass and the woods, from which Boone's family carved out their share of the colony of Pennsylvania. Runners who competed in the race shared a misery of their forefathers. As they bent over to catch their breath after the race, they discovered they were covered with ticks! Ankles, and legs were dotted with the foul insects, and body scans from family members were required in order spot and remove the jaws of the blood suckers from the limbs of exhausted race participants.

On Independence Day in 1976, I celebrated our nation's Bicentennial at Jersey Shore. No, not at the beach or at the site of the current reality television show, but at Jersey Shore, Pennsylvania.

Jersey Shore, Pennsylvania is located on the West Branch of the Susquehanna River, in Lycoming County, approximately fifteen miles west of Williamsport. From 1773 to 1785, a group of illegal settlers, squatters, called the Fair Play Men, established their own system of self-rule in the community. They staked their own claim on the land they settled, and, in an odd coincidence, they read their Declaration of Independence from Great Britain on July 4, 1776, under the Tiadaghton Elm tree on the banks of the Pine Creek, about three miles outside of Jersey Shore.

So, on July 4, 1976, the Tiadaghton Elm 10K took runners from the quiet village of Jersey Shore out to a huge tree, with a trunk the size of a small warehouse, and back. This was, allegedly, the very elm under which independence was declared in the north-central mountains of Pennsylvania, on the very day a similar, albeit more famous, document was signed in Philadelphia.

If you're a 'Baby Boomer,' you may recall the old ditty, "Camptown Races." I recall Bugs Bunny singing the song in one of his cartoons.

"Camptown ladies sing this song, Doo-dah! Doo-dah!

Camptown race track five miles long, Oh, doo-dah day."

The song was written in the 19th century by Bradford, Pennsylvania county resident, Stephen Foster.

Well, the Camptown Race really does exist, and, unlike many of the other races in this chapter, still exists today. In fact, the race celebrated its 44th anniversary this past September. Unlike the race of song, the real Camptown race is a 10K cross country race, held near the town that bears its name.

The race is a classic, real old-time cross country event. The course climbs up steep and winding hills, crosses creeks, and features rocky and rough terrain. Current race director, Karl Peterson, describes it perfectly when he calls the course, "absolutely grueling."

Like so many local races all over America, what the Camptown event lacks in number of participants (the race draws between sixty and eighty runners), it makes up for with quaint, small town hospitality. It is held in conjunction with a community festival. There's a kid's fun run, a hayride, chicken barbecue, along with booths manned by local vendors and artists.

One of the most interesting local races of the era was contested around the small village of Barnesville, in Pennsylvania's northern Schuylkill County. Until the mid-20th century, Barnesville was the home of the Lakeside Ballroom. Folks from all over the east coast would flock to Lakeside to listen and dance to the big bands of the area. It was also the site of Lakewood Park, a sprawling, wooded area, which featured a large swimming pool, a roller coaster, carousel, and a miniature train.

In the 1970s, though, each July, for two weeks, some 30,000 visitors a day would flock to the defunct park site, as it was transformed into the Bavarian Festival, a German beer fest and ethnic celebration, featuring oom-pah-pah bands and folks in lederhosen.

For several years, festival organizers added a 20K race to their schedule of events. The event was nothing short of masochism. Held in mid-July, the twelve-plus mile course was fit for a mountain goat. There was not a flat spot along the entire route. In addition, shade and water were in short supply. Runners who survived and stumbled back to the site of the former amusement park, and the shady finish area often made their way back to the giant beer hall, where copious quantities of beverages were usually consumed.

The Running Boom featured many unique and challenging events. I had the momentary absence of common sense to take on one such challenge in June 1977.

On a track near Reading, Pennsylvania, nine teammates and I joined eleven other teams in a 24-hour relay race.

From 6:00 p.m. on Friday to 6:00 p.m. on Saturday, each runner would run a mile, and then pass to the next participant on the team. Since the team consisted of ten members, one would, theoretically, run about one mile each hour.

My teammates and I were all near the top of our running games, so our times were fast, with each runner turning in mile times less than five minutes. As each hour went by, however, attrition began to set in. We slogged through the cool June evening and greeted the hot and humid new dawn. With six hours to go, we were down to six runners. Injury and fatigue began to assassinate remaining competitors. The infield and bleachers began to resemble a military field hospital. By the time we finished, my team had dwindled to four runners. I had run twenty-eight miles, and as a team we had covered 267 miles, 1,365 yards, which earned us a plaque a little larger than a postage stamp and a state record. I also earned a knee injury that put me on the shelf for several weeks. I have been unable to ascertain if the record still stands. Given that the race was one of those crazy ideas of the Boom era, I doubt the event has been contested frequently in the last thirty plus years.

Cash prizes for racing were scarce in the '70s and '80s, but amusing forms of race awards were abundant.

At a race attended by Randy Haas and me, sponsored by a local beer company, the tall trophies were enveloped by a beer can. Randy won the race, so he received, naturally, a larger trophy, encased by a larger can. As Haas returned with his award, spectators at the ceremony heard the distinct crinkle of aluminum as Haas, extremely disappointed with a prize he viewed as a chintzy arts and crafts project, displayed his runner's strength by crushing the beer can in frustration.

Often, at local races, well-intentioned merchants would offer gift certificates to award winners. Runners would receive such prizes as a $5.00 gift certificate at the local plumbing supply store, or a $10.00 credit at the neighborhood florist. During the early days of the running boom, however, runners would travel two hours or more to attend a race. It was not practical for participants to purchase their PVC pipe from the local plumber, and they probably weren't going to come back to redeem their $5.00 off at the local hair salon.

A local race held near a huge apple orchard offered a nearby vendor's potato salad and white tube socks as prizes to division winners.

Some races allowed award winners to select their awards from a table, on which one could select valuable prizes, such as water bottles, running journals, T-shirts, and mugs. As the selection process wound down, those at the end of the line had only an array of headbands from which to choose.

I once received a specially designed paper weight as a prize.

A car dealership near Allentown, Pennsylvania sponsored a race, and as part of the post race entertainment a wrestling ring was erected. The feature match involved a very large man versus Victor the Bear. The bear won.

Over the years I've garnered enough coal trophies to get me through the next energy crisis.

And at a Turkey Trot near Reading, Pennsylvania, if one was especially lucky enough to win the random drawing after the race the prize was…a live turkey!

For the most part, the names of races reflected the town or region in which the race was conducted.

There's the Coal Cracker 10K, held annually in Shenandoah, Pennsylvania, in the heart of anthracite coal country.

Littitz, in Pennsylvania Dutch Country, features The Pretzel Twist Race. Pretzels are produced in that region of the state.

Mifflinburg, at one time, was the buggy capital of Pennsylvania, at a time when horse-drawn buggies were the main mode of transportation in America. They once held the Buggy Museum 5K.

Reading, Pennsylvania, used to conduct the Pagoda Race. From downtown Reading, runners climbed a grueling hill to the turnaround point on Mount Penn, where a giant pagoda sits atop the hill, some 866 feet above the city.

Reading has no sizeable Asian population, so why the pagoda?

In the early 1900s, a Reading quarry owner, William Witman, decided to build the structure, which was inspired from a postcard from the Philippines, in an effort to cover the scars his quarries had left on the mountain. As one approaches, the pagoda, illuminated at night, serves as an oriental beacon guarding the city of Reading.

Other interesting races during the Boom era included the following events: The Slavic Run, Bear Chase, Indian Trail Half

Marathon, the Pungo Strawberry Festival 5K, Lung Run, the Chevy Chase (another car dealership), The Grand Ole Flag 5K, Eckley Miners Village 10K, The Roaring Creek 10K, the Turkey Run Five-Miler (not a turkey run, but in the town of Turkey Run), the Irish Jubilee, numerous races that began with "Saint," as they benefitted local churches, an abundance of 'firecracker' events around the Fourth of July, and the Mertztown Christmas Classic, as well as many other "Christmas" and "Frostbite" events during the month of December.

Many races of the '70s and '80s have disappeared. Some of the good ones have remained. Entry fees for these races were cheap, and T-shirts were plentiful. Eventually, a race, within an hour's distance, could be found on virtually any weekend. Most of these events were small, fifty to one hundred-fifty participants, but they were collegial. Rivalries were formed, and friendships were made.

Today there are fewer races, the fields are larger, and the entry fees are steeper. Similar to the early days of sandlot baseball, the races of the Boom era were the precursors of our modern mega races.

MILE 7–RUNNING BOOM: PART DEUX

The early years of the 21st century have produced another "running boom" in America.

In the mid-1970s, millions of Americans took up running and road races sprung up in cities, towns and villages all across the land. Jim Fixx wrote, *The Complete Book of Running,* and it instantly became a best seller. Innovations in training, footwear, and running clothing enabled an entire generation of Americans to hit the roads like never before

The running boom peaked in the late 1980s. "Boomers" got older, some gave up exercising, others moved toward triathlons or other forms of cross training, but most Americans just got fat. A society with a short attention span searched for shortcuts to fitness.

Ironically, as study after study describes us as an overweight nation, with dangerous levels of Type II Diabetes and heart disease that are straining our health care resources, it appears that America is actually experiencing another running boom.

Indeed, is perplexing. It may be similar to the fact that, in tough economic times, Americans seem to have more luxury items than ever.

There are not as many small, local races dotting the landscape of America, but mega-races abound, and trying to enter them is like trying to score the hottest ticket in town.

The sheer numbers have become staggering. More than 40,000 participants run in the New York City Marathon. The Chicago Marathon tops 45,000 runners, and, in the most bizarre twist of running irony, the venerable Boston Marathon, which had always boasted of its stringent qualifying times, closed its registration for the 2011 race in less than eight hours, with more than 30,000 participants.

Completing the grueling 26.2 mile distance has become more popular than ever in the United States. Statistics compiled at the end of 2009 indicate that nearly 468,000 men and women finished marathons in the U.S., an increase of 43,000 from 2008. In 2009, 397 marathons were held in the United States.

Races like the Peachtree Road Race, in Atlanta draw over 30,000 runners. San Francisco's famous Bay to Breakers road race routinely draws 70,000 to 80,000 participants, and is recognized by the Guinness Book of World Records as the world's largest footrace, having drawn more than 110,000 runners back in 1985.

In the tiny hamlet of Berwick, Pennsylvania, famous for its state championship football teams and its nuclear power plant, on Thanksgiving Day 2009, at the 100th running of the Berwick 9-mile Run for the Diamonds, a record field of 1,800 runners completed the course.

The new running boom is very different from the original. Runners are older and slower, and there are many more of them.

The largest percentage of male participants at the marathon distance consists of members of the 40-44 age group. For the women, the 25-29 age group leads the percentage of racers, but the number of women racers has dramatically increased since the first running boom.

The new boomers may be a bit plump, or less gaunt than the original boomers. Statistically, race participation has increased fourfold since the mid-80s, but today's runners are more concerned with overall fitness rather than race performance.

Many runners today race for charitable causes, such as the Susan B. Komen Race for the Cure, or Team in Training, which benefits the Leukemia & Lymphoma Society. Others participate in order to take control of their own lives, by losing weight or reducing stress

Olympic Marathon Champion, Frank Shorter, recently weighed in on the issue of the new running boom.

"All the advancements in technology - computers, the Internet, e-mail - that were supposed to free everyone up just has everyone working more." Shorter said. "Isn't it nice that running allows you to say at a certain point, 'I'm turning off the computer, turning off the cell phone, and I'm going out running for an hour. I'm doing it for me.' "

Indeed, our technology-dominated world has, in many ways, created a more complex lifestyle. Running provides a much-needed, simple method of exercise as well as a means of escape from emails, text messages, and phone calls.

Early 21st century America has distinguished itself with those unscrupulous cads who exploit the masses in pursuit of quick riches. Frivolous lawsuits abound as people seek a quick path to wealth. Lotteries are bigger than ever. Reality television has permitted talentless fools to bask in their fifteen minutes of fame. Sleazy politicians, news organizations with agendas, and, of course, our social networking outlets have enabled Americans to expose themselves, unabashedly, like never before. There are no shortcuts, there is no 'spin,' there is no 'bullshit' meter when it comes to running a race. The gun goes off, and the clock starts, and one may as well be naked. The runner is exposed to himself and his fellow competitors. It is both primal and pure. The rewards are simply: one's final time and the finish line.

Despite gloomy predictions of an obese, out-of-shape America, many folks have chosen a healthy path, as the new running boom has illustrated.

Road racing is a great equalizer, and every finisher is a winner.

In a stressful world, completing a race offers a unique sense of accomplishment. Today, more and more people are able to boast, "I finished a marathon."

The new running boom is the perfect prescription for America's mental and physical fitness.

MILE 8–RUNNING LOG

All runners should keep a daily account of their workouts.

Since 1975 I have kept a running log, a rather obsessive record of my running history for that particular day. Nothing fancy, my running logbook is often no more than a free daily planning book, usually obtained from an insurance agent, a company desiring my business, or as an incentive to buy a magazine. Remaining 'old school,' I have resisted spreadsheets or computer storage, keeping a copious written running diary for the past thirty-five years.

My running logs reside within a shelf of a desk in my living room. Two of them, this year's and the previous one, remain handy as I examine and compare my workouts from this year to last.

Each daily entry includes the weather conditions at the time of the workout, the course and distance, as well as the overall time, and, sometimes, mile splits. Often, an editorial comment is inserted, such as, "bitter cold," "very sore legs," or "terrible race."

A running log enables a runner to track progress, keep workouts that are beneficial, while scrapping those that aren't. When one sustains an injury, going back through a list of recent workouts can help to pinpoint the cause of the ailment.

One's running log entries may be brief or have the flair of a Russian novelist. Some runners list their weight, before and after the workout, resting pulse rate, their training partners, as well as a narrative of the workout. As a runner, one can actually modify time itself, as some runners choose to begin their training week on a Monday rather than on a Sunday, thereby stacking in their miles for the previous week by being able to compile more mileage on the weekends.

While some waited for the Y2K meltdown or some cataclysmic event as the new millennium approached, I spent New Year's Eve 1999 tallying the running mileage I compounded in the last quarter century of the millennium. The figure was 101,290 miles, more than most of the cars I've owned in my lifetime. As I wrapped up the year 2010, the number had grown to 116,319 miles.

Some folks celebrate or drown their sorrows with a few drinks; runners do so by grinding out miles on the road. My running log tells me where and how many joyous miles I ran on the days my three children were born, and the grieving miles I logged on the day my dad died.

My logbook chronicles the summer day in 1979 when I was ambushed by two dogs, distracted by one, then bitten on the hind quarter by the other. It reminds me of the streak of five-hundred thirty-eight consecutive days of training I compiled in 1983 and 1984. The pages talk about blizzards, hurricanes, blast furnace heat and bone numbing cold.

On July 1, 1987, I had a cyst removed from my upper back. The stitches hurt like hell, but I still managed a fifteen-mile run that afternoon.

Most runners love to run on sunny, pleasant, low humidity days, when temperatures hover in the 60s and 70s. One such day was September 11, 2001. I ran seven miles that day, by myself, thankful for all I had, my heart aching for the lives lost in a senseless act of terror against America.

In the chilly, predawn hours of November 7, 1989, I ran four miles in the dark at 5:30 a.m. before working at the polls all day. Around 9:00 p.m. that evening, I was elected mayor of the city of Pottsville.

During the Blizzard of '93, on March 13 and 14, I trudged through twenty-four inches of snow and endured forty to fifty-mile per hour winds during very slow four mile runs. On February 10, 2010, Eric Anchorstar and I toured the city streets at a snail-like twelve-minute per mile pace, through a storm that dumped more than thirty inches of snow on our region.

There are few entries in my logs describing treadmill runs. Until about five years ago I had NEVER run on a treadmill. I may be a purist, but a great part of having a love affair with running is having actually experienced a blizzard, torrential rain, or Arctic-like cold. Most runners have heard the phrase, "You're crazy for running outside on a day like today." Maybe it takes us back to our caveman roots or our pioneer heritage, but most runners feel good about confronting nasty weather and living to tell about it.

Treadmills have their place, and are beneficial in many ways, but for most runners, the road under the soles provides the ultimate satisfaction.

With two miles to go on an eight- mile run on May 13, 2000, I felt a dull ache on the top of my left foot. The pain increased for the next mile, reducing me to a walk. I made it home and awoke the next morning astonished to find my left foot twice the size of the right, hideously swollen. Inexplicably, I had broken the third metatarsal. I endured a cast up to my knee, and for the longest period in my adult life, my running log remained blank for the next thirty-nine days.

A running log can be a history of one's running life, both good and bad. It can be a guidepost, a road map for future training, or a terrific slice of nostalgia. In short, it's a "Dear Diary" of running, training, and racing. It is a written testimony of accountability to oneself

It doesn't matter whether you started training last week or last century; whether you're fast or slow, a running log is an essential tool for every road warrior.

Recession, war, personal tragedy or triumph, sorrow or joy, the runner's logbook stands as both a solid anchor and a safe port at which to dock at each workout's end.

MILE 9–SEASONS

Most of the United States, and, indeed, many parts of the globe, lie within the humid continental climate zone. For those of us who conduct most of our workouts outdoors this simply means that, when it comes to weather, anything goes.

Today one can escape unsuitable weather conditions by retreating to the safe, warm confines of the treadmill, but there is something noble, exciting, and gratifying about going eyeball to eyeball with Mother Nature and causing her to blink.

We have come a long way since the early days of the running boom. Running gear has graduated from bulky sweatshirts and nylon running suits of days gone by, to high tech fabrics that keep us warm and dry in the cold, while keeping us cool in the heat. Rain and snow are repelled by waterproof shells, socks, and shoes. Today's running gear technology has enabled us to run comfortably in virtually every weather condition.

The ultimate challenge for runners occurs during the winter months. Depending upon where you live, this season might hang around for two or three months, or as many as six or seven months. Proper preparation is the key to surviving this brutal time of the year, and a delicate balance must be achieved in order to maintain maximum comfort as well as safety.

Non-runners cannot possibly understand the amount of body heat we generate when we train. After about a mile or so, our bodies have produced seven to ten times more body heat than produced at rest, enough heat to turn our bodies into a tropical paradise. The tricky wardrobe decision for most runners is determining how to stay warm but not too warm. Water has a cooling effect, so too much sweat will steal precious body heat. Unlike the warm months, where dressing for a run is relatively simple, each run in cold conditions requires careful thought.

Base layers need to be dry. That means socks, underwear, gloves and hats must be made from one of the new dry woven fabrics.

Mittens are warmer than gloves, as they do not separate the fingers and the heat produced. Yes, forty percent of the body's heat is lost through the head; so on the coldest days, a hat is a necessity.

Even severe cold can be dealt with. The runner's main winter enemy is, however, wind. Wind manages to upset the delicate balance of power between heat and cold. Body temperatures, regulated to provide maximum warmth, are robbed by the wind. Dress too warmly and the sweat will feel like icy daggers that penetrate flesh when the gusts strike. On a windy winter's day it is always advisable to choose an out and back course. Run into the wind before sweat accumulates, then enjoy a tailwind on the way home. It makes sense both physically and psychologically. On the way home, a bitter wind chill is negated. Take cover if possible. A grove of trees, the blockade afforded by running behind a mountain, even the canyon between tall buildings, anything to prevent the icy enemy from gathering speed in an open area and slicing through the warm cocoon of running your gear.

Dangerous wind chills may pose a frostbite threat to exposed skin. Therefore, use lots of petroleum jelly on the face, and lip balm on the lips. Eat more before you run, as the body is working very hard simply to cook up enough heat in order to keep you alive out there. Male runners should guard private parts. An extra layer of shorts is a good idea. If the tips of your fingers have ever become numb from the cold, you have a very good grasp of the pain you endured when they began to thaw out. Well . . . imagine applying that pain to your male member. It is not fun.

The lack of humidity during the winter months could chap the tail of an alligator. It will do the same to your skin, so keep yourself moisturized. Skin cracks on the feet are particularly bothersome. Keep them greased up. Also, those nice hot showers we like after we run are not good for winter worn skin. Towel off and take fewer showers. Your loved ones may not appreciate it, but your skin will.

Ice and snow can both be a nuisance as well as a danger to runners. Our running shoes, ideal for gripping the ground below us, are fine for maintaining traction on snow, but the raised soles act like b.b.'s on the ice. Be extremely careful on icy sidewalks and streets. Icy days are treadmill days.

Winter is a great time to actually boost your weekly mileage. Don't worry about quality miles, though. Slog it out, be careful, and build up the miles as well as your aerobic capacity.

Few training venues are more sensory than running on a secluded trail after a freshly fallen snow. The still silence is broken only by the crunch of running shoes on the virgin surface. Puffs of carbon dioxide are expelled with each exhaled breath. The steam dissipates in the still air. Colors are few. A sunny, blue sky or a steel gray one, meshes with the brown remains of deciduous trees or the deep teal of evergreens. Everywhere you look, the world is a glistening white: beneath feet, clinging to trees, covering rocks and earth, as if to cover all its impurities. Introducing a runner to this scene is like superimposing a life into a still picture.

Throughout my running career, although I detest winter weather, I have consistently run more miles in January than I have in June. There's something about the winter, the lack of other activities and the cabin fever that drives a runner outside for that daily run. June, with its many other activities, sometimes winds up being a more difficult time to train, as there are many other things going on. We northerners believe winter makes you a tougher runner.

Runners should celebrate, like the ancient pagans, December 21 or 22, the day of the Winter Solstice. Darkness is another major winter enemy of runners. It limits the available amount of safe hours in which one can train. Decreased visibility is threatening to runners. Since we share our roads with two-thousand pound objects made of steel that travel at greater speeds than we, it is imperative that all runners wear something reflective when running at dawn, dusk, or in the dark. Plan your daily route on streets which allow good footing. After a constant descent in the amount of daylight, the Winter Solstice begins the process of additional minutes of light that continues until the Summer Solstice, some six months later. Throughout those months of darkness, however, runners must remain cautious and vigilant.

As the sun rises higher in the sky and the days become longer, runners shed upper garments, bare their legs, and the sights and smells of spring appear. Spring in Pennsylvania is often a schizophrenic season. A gorgeous seventy-degree day is followed a windy day in the thirties. Cold, forty-degree rainy days penetrate the bones, sometimes forcing one to long for the good old days of winter, and those dry, cold spells.

Spring smells good. Geese begin their northern migration, there are more sounds in the air, times are faster, and everything looks brighter. Workouts seem easier, as the physical and psychological effects of winter melt like ice in the warm sun.

The first few warm days of spring unleash an array of interesting characters who, perhaps, are just now beginning to cash in on their New Year's resolution, or have looked in the mirror and noticed a few extra pounds.

As the temperature spikes into the sixties they appear: guys without shirts, young moms with their baby joggers, their sons and daughters wondering what's going on in their worlds, members of local track teams, hoping their coaches won't spot them walking instead of running. There's the headband brigade, the folks carrying hand weights that look like weapons, all shapes and sizes, old and young. Most of these folks won't be around in another month, but they are the annual denizens of spring.

Spring is the time for runners to get back on the track. No matter how fast you run, speed work is an integral part of your training. When the weather breaks and the snow melts it's time to regain some of the speed that has remained dormant over the winter months. It's fun to get the legs moving quickly again. Even the smell of an all-weather track provides a mental boost to most runners.

Some runners hate summer more than winter. I am not one of them. Their adage is, "You can dress for cold, you can't dress for heat." Good point I guess. Still, I hate cold.

Just as wind is the most difficult part of winter, humidity is the summer foe of runners. Humidity is relative. Is that why they call it, "relative humidity?" A humid day in Pennsylvania is not a humid day in Florida. In 1986, I committed the ultimate 'snowbird' mistake. I left the frigid Pennsylvania winter to compete in Miami's Orange Bowl Marathon. The race was held in February, it began at dawn, so my logic was, "How hot could it be?" About half way through the race I had my answer. Temperatures hit the high seventies, with eighty percent humidity. I struggled to the finish line in shoes so wet it felt as though I had run some of the miles in the ocean.

For the most part, avoiding intense summer heat is easy. Run early in the morning, in the evening, or find shade. Wooded trails that comprise some of my training courses are sometimes ten to fifteen degrees cooler than courses that are in the direct sunlight. Water has a cooling effect, so running close to the beach is not as hot as running inland.

Conversely, for those of you who run in desert climates, running can be magnificent. Now, I realize that one-hundred-ten degree heat is brutal, with or without humidity, but hot and dry can be fun. In 1984, I ran for three consecutive days as I was passing through Albuquerque, New Mexico. Each day I ran past a bank thermometer that read 'one-hundred degrees.' The humidity hovered at an arid ten-percent. It felt like seventy-five degrees. When I finished, I was caked in salt.

For all summer runners, everywhere, hydration is the key. We can never drink enough water. The pee test is still the best. The darker your pee, the more dehydrated you are. Don't underestimate the need to remain hydrated. Severe dehydration can mean death to a runner. That couple of pounds you lose at the end of a summer training run is primarily water weight which needs to be replenished. Remember to drink BEFORE you run, and if you're doing a long run, 'plant' some water along the course. After the run, continue to replenish your fluids.

Most runners enjoy a cold, adult beverage on occasion, and, indeed, a cold beer after a workout is quite refreshing. Keep in mind, however, alcohol dehydrates an already dehydrated body. So, enjoy responsibly, but make sure you consume plenty of water as well.

John Ausherman has been a top notch runner since the late 1970s. Ten years ago, however, he experienced, first hand, the deadly power of heat and humidity.

One of John's favorite training courses is an eleven-mile mountain trail near his home, at a State Park, in Chambersburg, Pennsylvania. Being a veteran runner, John planned his workout for the early evening in order to avoid the heat of the day. Near the end of the run on an eighty-degree, humid evening, he began to feel dizzy. The last mile of the course was a blur, as he staggered incoherently to the finish. He collapsed and, luckily, was immediately taken to the local hospital's emergency room. His body temperature boiled at one hundred five degrees, not far from death. After some confusion, he was given intravenous fluids and his temperature was decreased. He has developed a healthy fear and respect of the potential damage that can be wrought by heat and humidity.

Another potential killer during the summer months is the thunderstorm. Precautions may be taken for most other weather conditions, but there is only one sure fire way of staying safe during a thunder and lightning event: don't run!

In an open area, lightning will strike a tall object, such as a runner. Leaves on trees are excellent conductors of electricity, so don't seek shelter there. Lying flat in a ditch may save one from a lightning strike, but even that option is often not feasible. In addition, one may avoid being struck by a lightning bolt, but objects near you could be hit, causing you harm. The good news is that thunderstorms often pass quickly, so use the extra time to warm up or stretch, but don't gamble with this arm of Mother Nature.

Autumn may be the finest time of the year for runners. Humidity dissipates, as if a blanket has been lifted from the atmosphere, mornings and evenings are cool, and races abound. In most parts of the country, the striking colors and shades of autumn are brilliant. Along roads and trails, runners enjoy an explosion of autumnal beauty, as the trees gasp for life before winter cold strips them of their leaves. It is a perfect time of the year to train for a marathon, cross country races, or the many other events on the race calendar. Hats, gloves, long sleeved shirts, and tights gradually make their appearance, and, for a while, feel good. By February, however, they are reduced to a burdensome annoyance.

Being a runner heightens one's appreciation of the four seasons, and deepens one's respect for nature's power. There's a certain charm in ending a training run and displaying two-toned legs. You know, light colored in front, and caked in mud on the back. Dodging the thick raindrops during a torrential downpour is exciting. Thawing out when the temperatures dip below zero provides a sense of accomplishment that regular mortals fail to experience. Finishing a run and watching the sweat pour like an open faucet over you, or the feeling of jumping into a swimming pool, or, better still, the ocean, after a summer training session is something only we, as runners, can truly appreciate.

The clock is ticking. We have been allocated a finite number of seasons on this planet. But we have chosen to make the most of them. Do it! Get out there when the temperatures are frigid. Tell the wind to "bring it on," defeat the heat, and enjoy the days that are picturesque gems.

Dress properly. Eat healthy foods to fuel the fire. Drink liberally. Water is your friend. Don't ignore warning signs. Be daring but not foolish.

Make every day, week, and year your season in the sun.

MILE 10–OMG!

Wayne Parfitt was an excellent high school runner. In 1983, he ranked as one of the top 3200- meter high school harriers in our local region. Short, with powerful legs, he loved to train by running long distances. High school tracks and cross country courses seemed confining to him, as they limited his ability. He craved longer races, as his diminutive stature and dogged work ethic were well suited for the marathon distance.

Upon graduation from Pottsville Area High School Wayne decided to take a year off before pursuing his higher education. He also, at the age of eighteen, made the commitment to become a marathon runner.

Parfitt and I trained together during the summer and the fall, often logging ninety to one-hundred mile training weeks. I ran the New York City Marathon; while he continued to train for the Philadelphia Marathon, which was contested a month later.

Parfitt's goal was to break two-hours, fifty-minutes, which was then the qualifying mark for open division participants at the Boston Marathon. I agreed to pace him for as long as I could, and as the miles rolled by at the Philadelphia Marathon, it soon became apparent that his months of hard work had paid off. From the start in suburban Ambler, and as the race made its way into the city, the young runner was zeroing in on a possible sub-2:40 marathon time.

Feeling remarkably recovered from my race at New York City, I was able to keep pace with Wayne the entire way. As he neared the finish line at Independence Hall, the crowd cheered wildly at the sight of this determined young man, knees smashing the air, teeth clenched, arms pumping rhythmically.

The frenzied applause and ear-piercing cheers reached a crescendo as Parfitt's toe collided with the finish line. Then, like a bottle of champagne on New Year's Eve, emotions, nerves, and the previous night's dinner exploded into the crowd, as, with a turn of his head, the runner who had just turned in an incredible time of 2:39:39, projectile vomited into the onlookers, transforming the chorus of, 'Yeas,' into a hideous strain of 'Eewwws.'

Running and racing have a way of eroding inhibitions, as sometimes necessity dictates. Intense caloric burn keeps a runner's engine running hot during a workout, so running around scantily clad, in all kinds of weather, is the norm. Besides, shirts can be bothersome. Just ask the legions of runners who have suffered from 'BNS,' bloody nipple syndrome. Since few of us gentlemen wear sports bras, this condition is, generally, a male runner's problem.

Sweating and cooling cause the body to react, and I'm sure there's some medical explanation for it, but that's of little consequence. Many runners have completed races only to gaze downward to see two red rivulets that look like a leaking crimson magic marker, emanating from their nipples. For most runners, the condition looks bad, and may be a bit embarrassing, but is relatively painless . . . for a while. The initial post-race BNS shower is not a pleasant experience. That first, exhilarating spray of water stings the affected areas, like salt in a wound. Attempting to reenter the real world, where folks actually wear shirts is a challenge, as the raw nipples are, literally, an irritation.

BNS is a real possibility when one is running a marathon. Runners fear overheating so, often, a singlet is worn as the sole upper garment. At my first marathon in Harrisburg, my mother was in attendance. Her biggest shock of the day came when I removed my shirt after the race, revealing nipples covered with band aids, crisscrossed to form an "x" over each nipple.

When training or racing, use band aids, petroleum jelly, or the non-greasy glides on the market now, in order to ensure good nipple health.

Chafing, particularly in the crotch and under the arm pits, is both annoying and painful. Grease up those areas, especially in humid weather.

Spectators at a race are treated to a bouquet of smells emanating from the crowd of runners, especially in the summer time.

Menthol creams, rubs, and balms mix with sweaty bodies to create a delight for the nose only a visit to a sewage treatment facility could match. To combat the foulness a sweaty body creates, runners often go a little heavy on the deodorant stick, which sometimes produces a lathery arc, resembling the head of a fine German beer, oozing from beneath the armpits of many a racer.

There's one sure fire method of identifying a runner. No, it's not the gaunt appearance of a prisoner of war, it's the feet.

Before my daughter Kelly became a runner, she revealed to me that my gnarly feet were a source of trauma to her as a youth. Since that revelation, each time I glance at my feet I understand her point. Actually, it's not so much the feet as the toes. The people on the beach who have toenails painted black or purple, they are runners, and their toenails aren't painted. I usually own two or three non-colored toenails, but, sometimes, after a marathon, all my toenails are Gothic. There are calluses everywhere. Partial toenails set at various angles at the top of my toes, as do the toes themselves, pointing in different directions, like the hands of a clock. Some of the toenails haven't quite exited my body, so another grows over top. In the cold, dry Pennsylvania winters, tiny fissures form, which are the equivalent of paper cuts on the feet. I perform surgery, slicing nails, lancing blisters, and draining blood from under nails, which, after a twenty six-mile race are in the same condition as a thumbnail having been struck by a hammer. My wife has performed pedicures, wrapped my feet, and has even filed nails, but it's an occupational hazard of the sport. If you're going to be a runner you better give up your dreams of becoming a foot model.

Another disgusting, but often necessary habit of runners is 'snurching.' Now, most runners, male and female need to spit during a run, but snurching is another one of those male tendencies. Nasal passages get stuffed up, so a standard snurch involves placing an index finger on the outside of the nostril, followed by a good hard blow. Although snurch by-products sometimes fail to clear one's own body or clothing, courtesy dictates that one avoids snurching on a fellow runner.

Then, there are the bodily functions.

Whether one has just begun to train or has run for decades, keeping bodily functions in check at the proper time is a constant struggle.

The New York City Marathon boasts "the world's largest urinal.' The trough, which extends for several hundred yards, funnels the urine of thousands of male runners, who line up, side by side, for hours prior to the start of the race. The preponderance of potties, however, never seems to be adequate, as, upon crossing the Verrazano Bridge, hundreds of runners are lined up against a wall, relieving themselves, near the two- mile mark in the race.

At the 2010 Boston Marathon, I locked into a pace with another local runner. Our finishing goals were the same, so we paced each other for half the race. I noticed that he drank a great deal of water at each water station. The temperatures hovered in the fifties, so I wondered why he felt the need to hydrate so frequently. Around the fourteen-mile mark of the race he vanished. I didn't think he'd sprint away without a farewell, so I was perplexed. Hours after the race he phoned to tell me that the water forced him to visit the job johnny, a few yards off the course. By the time he got back and settled into a pace, the pit stop had cost him several minutes.

At the starting line of many races, runners, both male and female often drop to one knee or squat. This is not a prayer ritual or some pre-race routine. It is one final relief prior to the gun. Hundreds of pairs of expensive, finely designed, colorful running shoes are enveloped by the streams of urine that flow past moments before the race begins.

If you have a loved one or friend who suffers from chronic constipation, tell them to start running. Being a runner gives a new meaning to being a 'regular' guy. During my many years in the sport, my running partners and I have covered hundreds of thousands of topics during our workouts, but constipation has never been one of them. Simply said, runners are prolific poopers.

Ducking behind a tree to urinate is one thing, but squatting for a bowel movement is a little much. For runners, though, when the urge strikes, far from home, it can be devastating.

Brian Tonitis and I were cruising through a ten-mile training run one summer day when he exclaimed, "Go a half mile up and come back for me bud." His desperate sprint into some thick vegetation explained his absence. I ran ahead for a few minutes, and when I returned, he was wearing one sock!

On a blistering hot summer morning near Virginia Beach I set out on an eight-mile training run. In 'no man's land,' far from the start of my run, the urge struck. At a construction site I spied a job johnny. Quickening my pace I entered the chamber and locked the door. The temperature inside must have been one hundred thirty-degrees. Thanks to the boiling remains of other visitors, that experience ranks as one of the vilest of my entire life.

Randy Haas has been known to carry a neat little paper towel square in the waistband of his running shorts, in case an emergency should arise during a workout. Occasionally, he exits a workout, temporarily, but returns, refreshed, and without his paper towel.

An anonymous runner I know ducked into the bushes only to discover, several days later, that his emergency foray into nature resulted in a nasty case of poison ivy on his posterior.

Near the starting line of the Boston Marathon in the quiet village of Hopkinton police patrol the woods prior to the start of the race, for the purpose of busting those who may be dropping their drawers for one final evacuation before the long journey to Boston. It is to no avail, however, as experienced runners wisely post a sentry while they take their toilet paper and duck behind a tree.

There is one universal truth about all races. There are NEVER enough job johnnies. At big city races I have shared back alley toilets with homeless people. Once I witnessed a brilliant sunrise as I squatted behind some sea oats near an Atlantic Beach before a 5K race.

Mercifully, I have never 'fumbled' during a race. One of the greatest female runners of all time, the late Grete Waitz, did, however, lose control of her bowels during the New York City Marathon. She still won the race.

Chafing, bloody nipples, an upset stomach, ugly feet, snurching, and sharts are some of the pitfalls of our sport. If you're a runner, you've experienced some or all of these afflictions. There is no magic solution to any of these potential problems. World class runners and beginners alike share these afflictions. Part of becoming a better runner is to become better prepared, for both training runs and races. Know how much water to drink. Avoid foods that will make your bowels gripe. I always enjoy a good salad, but I never eat one before I run because I have a difficult time digesting it. Lube up: coat your crotch, pits, and the tips of your toes.

If you're not a runner, you're probably repulsed by the things you've read in this chapter. If not, you ARE a runner . . . or should be.

MILE 11–E-I-E-I-O

The Tumbling Run Road is an unforgiving ribbon of blacktop, an undulating series of hills, located south of Pottsville. My running partners and I have chosen the narrow, hilly swath of road as a site for our long training runs for many years.

In the early 1980s I set out on a twenty-miler in preparation for the New York City Marathon. The late summer temperature was warm, and the humidity hung like a thick, invisible fog under the canopy of maple and oak trees that line the route. Hills had begun to take their toll, and I counted three remaining over the final five miles. Rounding a curve, I saw a moving figure a quarter mile ahead. It was the unmistakable gait of a runner. My pace quickened. Few runners can resist the thrill of the hunt. At the base of a steep, one hundred fifty-yard grade, I drew close. Suddenly my prey, Charlie Stock, a friend and local runner, whose long red hair and round, horned rimmed glasses gave him the look of a sixties' rock star, spun, startled, yelling, "AHHHHH," in the manner of a Banzai warrior. He stopped, clutched his chest, and breathing heavily said, "Jeez, I thought you were a bear."

Today, we still refer to the spot as the "Charlie Stock Hill."

Runners commune with nature every day. Unless your training is exclusively urban, you have encountered all kinds of animals at sometime during your daily runs. Trail running is an excellent way of truly being a part of nature, up close.

Several of my running partners have, unlike Charlie Stock, met up with real bears on their training runs. In our part of the country, black bears are prevalent. They are more afraid of us than we are of them, with one exception. A mother will go into a defensive mode if she perceives her cubs are threatened. Bears are faster than we are. They can swim and climb trees. If a bear comes after you, lay face down, play dead, and hope the mama isn't too angry or hungry. Say a prayer and hope.

On the Monday after Thanksgiving, over a million hunters descend upon the woods of Pennsylvania for the first day of white tail deer season. Anyone who has done a lot of running through the forests of Penn's Woods can assure the hunters they've come to the right place. Deer are magnificent creatures, and it is difficult for a runner not to appreciate their graceful manner. Sometimes a deer will stand, motionless, several feet away and watch runners pass. It's as if the animal is critiquing the runner's style. Startled, they will sometimes gallop away in a majestic manner, their sharp hooves barely touching the ground, making less noise than the squirrels.

Speaking of noise, wild turkeys abound in northeastern Pennsylvania. Encountering a flock, one is amused by their high-pitched cackle. If a bird has been surprised by a runner, it will strut away in a manner that would remind one of a comedian in the old black and white films of the 1920s.

Pheasants and woodcocks enjoy waiting until you nearly step on them before taking flight. Suddenly silence is punctuated by the frantic flapping of wings and an unusual squawk. It's enough to frighten even the bravest of runners.

Most folks in our part of the world enjoy watching a flock of geese course through the sky in a perfect formation, honking like it's a warning blast for oncoming objects.

Geese, however, can be nasty creatures. They have a way of, literally, soiling an area, as their feces are voluminous and strong. They don't like runners invading their space, and have been known to attack. Once a goose assaulted a local cyclist's white helmet, perhaps thinking it was a giant egg!

Not a whole lot to like about snakes. Like so many Americans, snakes like to sun themselves on hot summer days. Black snakes are common in our area, as are copperheads. Black snakes are not poisonous; copperheads are. Nature has provided snakes with an excellent natural camouflage, which is great for them, but bad for us. Our local coal silt-covered trails are like those black lava beaches of Hawaii for black snakes. My running partners and I have had numerous encounters with these creatures, which become invisible on the ebony ground. They stretch across the road, causing us to employ our questionable hurdling skills as we attempt to avoid stepping on them, something that would cause a painful outcome for us.

Recently, Tom Daugherty, a newcomer to long distance running, enjoyed a run on the Auburn Trail on a warm, early Spring afternoon. Lost in thought and listening to his iPod, he didn't notice the six-foot black snake enjoying the weather as it sunned itself, lazily stretched across the road. Startled, he clumsily avoided the creature, but hyper extended his right knee in the process. He was forced to walk the remaining two miles of his workout.

I've never known a runner who has been bitten by a snake. Most snake encounters we've had have occurred deep in the woods far from home. Snake venom coursing through a runner's rapidly pumping heart would probably not produce a good ending. My only advice here is: don't get bitten by a snake when you're running.

Woodchucks, or groundhogs, are prevalent in Pennsylvania. Yes, everyone enjoys watching cuddly Punxsutawney Phil as he makes his annual weather prediction from the town of the same name. Groundhogs are fat, brown, nasty creatures, that dig ankle-breaking holes and bare their razor-sharp teeth as runners approach. Getting bitten by one of these creatures would be painful, and possibly rabies-producing.

Little creatures of the woods sometimes evoke 'Charlie Stock' moments, as they seemingly appear out of nowhere, scurrying by, rustling dried leaves and branches in their wake. Squirrels, chipmunks, rabbits, raccoons and possums often become annoyed when two-legged animals invade their space.

One of the greatest generals of all time, Alexander the Great, went undefeated on the battlefield. He was stabbed, slashed, and thrown from his horse, but lived to fight another day. It was the tiny malaria-carrying mosquito that killed him, after he had conquered the world, at the age of thirty-three.

Mosquitoes, biting flies, gnats and stinging insects of all types can create misery for runners.

Six years ago, on a warm May morning, I set out on a seven-mile run. Three miles along, a flying insect flew in my face. As I swatted it away, it stung me on the upper lip, causing me to utter a string of profanities. As I continued to run with my friend Rob Crosswell, swelling caused great difficulty in my ability to talk. Rob glanced at me, exclaiming, "That looks pretty bad." Upon finishing the workout at The Stump, I glanced at my image in a car window. What looked back at me was a boxer who had been on the losing end of a round with Mike Tyson. What's more, I talked like I was still wearing a fighter's mouth guard. My lip had swelled to three times it size.

A trip to the emergency room revealed that a sting on the upper lip is sometimes prone to increased swelling due to the sinus cavity. A shot of an antihistamine and, within a couple of hours, the swelling subsided.

Alexander the Great I'm not, but being brought down by an insect is not fun.

Take precautions against these animals, as they are the ones that will cause you the most discomfort. Spray on mosquito repellent, wash off perfume or cologne, and be aware of heavy insect areas. Wear sunglasses when possible to keep bugs out of your eyes.

Dogs are loyal and lovable. They are, truly, man's best friend. Often, however, they are a runner's worst enemy. Being territorial creatures, they don't like to have their space intruded upon. Just ask the mailman. A runner in motion is always an invitation for a dog, to either give chase in play, or give chase to attack. Unfortunately, as runners, we are unaware of a dog's true intent. My two dogs are nearly as dear to me as my children. Sometimes, my wife contends that they are dearer to me then her. (Of course, she's wrong)

Dogs act instinctively, their actions fashioned by their genetic code. Dog owners, however, need to be more responsible. If one is running on someone's property and a dog attacks, in my view, the runner is at fault. Training on a public road or trail is a completely different story. A runner, when attacked, has every right to defend himself in any manner, and take whatever legal or civil action necessary to ensure that no further attacks occur.

As a runner, a dog bite is the last thing I expect to endure. As a dog owner, though, I have had the misfortune of witnessing the irresponsibility of a dog owner who allows his dog to roam free, and the consequences that result from that irresponsible action.

While running through the small town of Palo Alto a few years ago, a collie appeared out of nowhere, and began to run along with our group. It was playful, its long coat flapping in the breeze as it loped along. Suddenly it veered into the path of a vehicle and was struck. The poor animal lay on the street, injured, helplessly panting and whimpering. The driver was devastated. Soon, as we tried to attend to the animal, the owner appeared and took the collie home.

We felt bad, as though it was we who caused the dog to be hit, but the real culprit was the irresponsible pet owner.

I have screamed, karate-kicked at, and fended off attacking dogs with my fists. I have gotten in the face of dog owners. In all my years on the road, however, I have only been on the receiving end of a dog's fangs twice.

Back in the late 1970s, I was gliding along a downhill portion of the Hillside Road, three miles from my home. Suddenly, from across a huge front lawn charged a German Shepherd and a small mutt. Furious, I fronted the Shepherd, my eyes wide, fists clenched. It seems, though, he had created a diversion, as his little partner came at me from the rear, sinking his teeth into my right hind quarter.

Though my ass stung, my rage overtook me. The dogs fled, realizing that they were dealing with a clearly unstable human being. I sprinted to the owner's residence, ready to confront the dogs if they mounted another attack. Pounding on the door, I greeted the owner with a litany of epithets as he answered. He calmly listened as I vented and then asked my name. He disarmed me by stating, "Oh, I know your father." I calmed down. He assured me there would be no further attacks and apologized. His word was good. From that time, the dogs never bothered me or any other runners.

Later in the day I submitted to tetanus shot, from which I experienced a terrible reaction of flu-like symptoms for two days. I still bear the L-shaped scar on my right hind cheek.

For more than thirty years I successfully eluded numerous canine assaults.

Until the winter of 2011.

We're no strangers to Winter in northeast Pennsylvania, but the Winter of 2010-2011 was unusually cold, with frequent snow and ice storms. On a Saturday in January, I decided to take an easy four-mile run around my neighborhood, as major roads were snowy and slick. A light, feathery snow fell as I rounded a corner, onto a street devoid of vehicular traffic, a little more than a mile from home. My idyllic, relaxing run was shattered by the sight of two large creatures sprinting toward me. I recognized the dogs as Rhodesian Ridgebacks, beautiful, but big and very strong animals, whose ancestors originated in South Africa where they were used to hunt lions. They had me in their sights from two-hundred yards away, and reached me in a matter of seconds, with their owner hopelessly lagging behind. I stopped;

fronting them, hand extended, palm down. One of the brothers nipped at my gloved hand, and, as if to complete the set of ass-bookends, which was initiated more than thirty years ago, the other attacked my left buttock, inflicting four inch long incisor incisions. The owner, who had been walking them, without a leash, arrived, breathless and shocked . . . not by the fact his dog just took a piece of my ass, rather, he was shocked by the fact that I was running on such a day!

As the snow fell, I scratched my head, astounded by his stupidity. I yelled, "Your dog just bit me on the ass." He disagreed, so, there, in the middle of the street, I pulled down the left side of my running tights, revealing my pasty white ass and its two slash marks.

Apologies abounded, but then came a more shocking query. The dog owner asked if I could give him an idea of approximately what time I run each day so he could be sure his dogs didn't attack me again. I figured the little kids on bicycles, or the mothers who walk their babies in their strollers on his street should check in with him as well.

I guess I've beaten the odds, given the number of years I've run and the miles I've logged. Two dog bites aren't so bad. So, based on my success, here's my advice. When a dog attacks, stop. More often than not, they'll retreat. For me, yelling and letting the dog know you're crazier than he is, usually works. Recently, on one of our training runs, my running partner, Eric Anchorstar, was confronted by a large dog. Eric fronted him, put up his dukes and said, "C'mon, you wanna fight?" The dog hasn't chased us since.

Know your breeds. I own a Labrador Retriever and I believe the breed is genetically incapable of harm. Labs, however, love to play and they love to be close to people. Sometimes they like to be too close to people.

As I approached the finish of a seven-mile trail run, I spotted two people walking their dogs. I observed that the animals were yellow Labs, hence I harbored no fear of attack. Dixie, my chocolate Lab, however, mounts her version of an attack on me daily. If you've ever owned a Lab, you know what I mean. Her tail wags so hard, it shakes her entire hind quarters. She weaves in between my legs, whimpering, frantic to present me with a sock, underwear, a chew toy, or some other sign of affection. And so it was with my new Lab friend. As I approached, he ran toward me, quickly veering to my left, his broad body forming a horizontal hurdle at knee-height. We collided, and like a very ungraceful Superman, I flew through the air, screeching to a halt on the forest floor, hands and a knee bloodied. I was consoled with huge, sloppy licks to the face from the dog and with apologies from the owner.

Some runners and cyclists carry pepper spray with them. If you are familiar with an area where a dog lurks, pick up a stick to defend yourself.

Across the planet runners enjoy a unique perspective. Whether you encounter a bobcat in the mountains, a Gila monster roaming the desert, or dodge a jellyfish on the beach, we share our training grounds with an amazing array of creatures, large and small. Sometimes, coexisting with them can be a challenge, but it's part of our appreciation of, and our connection with nature, with which we have become an integral part.

Back in 1978, fellow runner Gary Comfort and I planned to organize our own race. We decided that the rural setting of the Tumbling Run Road would be an ideal site. In addition, Guers Dairy, a family-owned local business, specializing not only in milk, but in a delicious homemade iced tea drink that is the favorite of local citizens, offered its facilities as a staging area for the event.

Having run a few races, Gary and I wanted to work hard so that our race would not suffer from some of the same shortfalls as other local races. Our race would be rural and beautiful. But, out in the country, dogs could be a problem. The day before the race we visited the farms along the route, asking folks if they could tie up their dogs during tomorrow's race. They graciously agreed. We contacted the Pennsylvania State Police about traffic control. We were good to go. All potential course impediments were eliminated. Or so we thought.

The race, held in early March, began on a cold morning in the midst of a snow squall that reduced visibility. One hundred thirty runners lined up to begin the hilly, five-mile course. Dogs barked, but they were safely restrained. Runners were treated to views of lush, snow-covered farmlands, complete with dairy cattle grazing in the fields. Halfway into the race, runners passed a field of cows, enclosed within a fence consisting of two metal wires. At a height of four feet, the cows could lean their heads over the top wire and serve as silent spectators while this strange parade of men and women in brightly colored outfits invaded their world. The course wound into a loop, and the cows were about to receive an encore performance from the one hundred thirty-member cast.

The excitement was, apparently, too much. A bovine bunch decided to make a break for it. Lead runners had long passed, so runners toward the end of the pack witnessed three of the huge animals leap the fence like high jumpers, joining the runners on the road to the finish line. One runner recalled, "The cow was running next to me, hooves clomping on the blacktop. The ground shook. It was a huge animal. I'm sure it was my fastest mile of the race for me. Maybe my fastest mile ever!"

The cattle, not known for their endurance, raced for only a few hundred yards before oxygen debt did them in. No runners or cattle sustained any injuries. To this day, participants still talk about Schuylkill County's version of Pamplona, Spain's Running with the Bulls.

MILE 12–RUN 'TIL IT HURTS

Allow me to begin this chapter with a disclaimer. I am not a medical doctor and possess no formal medical training. My advice in this chapter is rooted in more than thirty-five years of running, and the inevitable consequences of it.

Running hurts. Most of the time it is a good hurt and the results of it are usually positive. But, as the addictive quality of the activity kicks in, most folks crave more mileage, and seek faster race times. These two factors strain the body and, sometimes, injuries result.

Tom Daugherty does not look like a runner. In his thirties, he works as a middle school music instructor and band director. Formerly weighing in at nearly two-hundred-fifty pounds, he decided to take control of his fitness by beginning a running program. His initial objective was to shed pounds. Real runners, to him, looked like underfed prisoners of war.

As he began his training program, however, two years ago, he enjoyed the feeling of increasing his daily mileage from the one to two miles he had been doing, to three or four miles a day, four times a week. Pounds began to melt away, and there were days when he ran on a trail near his home in Lebanon, Pennsylvania, that he would paint a bull's eye on the runner ahead of him and reel him in, passing the ill-fated target with a rush of ecstasy.

His weight plummeted to a healthy two hundred fifteen pounds, covering his six-foot, three-inch frame.

Still, it was not enough for this greedy man. He craved more running challenges, so he entered his first race, a modest, local 5K event. Like most runners, entering just one race is like eating one potato chip, so he continued to race, times decreasing each time he crossed the finish line. Five milers, 10K's, fell in his wake, until he finally decided to run a half marathon last fall. His training paid dividends, as he achieved and smashed his goal of a sub-two hour finishing time.

Now is when the "Rocky" music should play, and the "Hoosiers" theme should end the story. But this is running, and runners, at all levels, walk a tightrope. If you're feeling too good, you're probably not training hard enough. Train too much, and you're headed toward an injury. Training on a daily basis has dramatically increased your pain tolerance, so you push yourself because anything else would leave you feeling wimpy.

After the euphoria of his successful half marathon wore off, Daugherty began to experience heel pain. It began as an annoying ache and grew into pain that caused him to limp. His daily workout times ballooned. He dreaded lacing up his shoes, wondering when the pain would begin coursing through his foot. He felt tired, beaten. He took a day off here, two days off there, but things didn't improve. After several months he felt a pain radiating down his leg, from his knee to his calf.

In a short period of time, Tom Daugherty had developed from a casual jogger to a dedicated runner and racer, and once this metamorphosis takes place, injuries are a real fact of life. There is a good ending to this story, though. After a cortisone shot and a pair of orthotics, Tom is back on the roads, running pain-free. He's building up his mileage again and is looking forward to his next race.

Distance running releases endorphins which, supposedly, suppress pain impulses and allow one to continue the physical activity for an extended period of time. Simply stated, distance running creates an increased tolerance for pain, which can be both a blessing and a curse.

At the Boston Marathon a few years ago, one of the male runners experienced a sharp pain in his thigh during the final miles of the race. The pain intensified, but the gentleman continued to run, determined to finish the race. As he crossed the finish line, he collapsed with a fractured femur. Adrenaline and endorphins combined to create a morphine-like pain block in his upper leg that evaporated at the conclusion of the race.

The most serious injury of my career was a broken metatarsal, which I sustained in May of 2000. It required immediate casting and a diagnosis of six weeks of immobilization. After four weeks, my podiatrist removed the cast to take a look at the foot. He declared that the healing process had progressed ahead of schedule, and that he could probably completely remove the cast, but he wouldn't.

Perplexed and angry, I asked why. His response was, "If I remove the cast, you're going to try to run on this foot, and possibly damage it permanently." I was livid, but, in my heart I knew he was absolutely correct. As soon as I left his office I would have been plotting ways to get back out on the road as soon as possible.

Most runners are delusional when it comes to pain and injuries that may result. We truly believe we are invincible, and, although our ability to withstand pain is far superior to the average person, we exist in a constant state of paranoia, fearing that we will allow pain to defeat us.

Injuries come in many different forms, affecting runners in various ways, but there really is a fairly logical way of approaching most any injury and properly dealing with it.

At the bottom of the runner's injury pyramid is simple soreness. A speed workout, a long run, weightlifting, or playing another sport may often produce soreness that one may construe as an injury. An increased amount of stretching, a pain-relieving muscle balm, and ibuprofen should keep one from missing a workout.

The next level of hurt may strike a specific area, such as the knee, hamstring, back, or heel. It may be a specific sore spot that could produce pain during certain movements, and may hurt when the workout begins. The pain, however, dissipates as the workout progresses. All the above remedies, as well as ice therapy should help. During this type of injury, sensible training is the key. Reduce your mileage, try to run on soft surfaces, and stay away from hills. A day or two of rest may be necessary for the injury to completely heal.

At the top of the injury pyramid is the pain that increases as you run. As runners, we delude ourselves into thinking we are reducing ourselves to wimp status if we succumb to pain, but the simple fact is, if the pain increases during the activity, the activity is causing the injury. Stop immediately. Walk home if you have to, and take some time off. You may be able to turn to an alternative method of exercise, such as walking, cycling, or swimming. If the injury is not soft tissue (bone), get an X-ray. See a doctor and procure a diagnosis.

It all starts with the feet.

If you think you're a cheapskate, that's ok in all aspects of your running, or in your life for that matter, but NEVER be cheap when it comes to your running shoes. Running may be one of the most inexpensive sports, requiring little equipment. Do not risk injury with a cheap, or worn out pair of running shoes, and if you feel an injury approaching, begin your self-diagnosis by checking the wear of your shoes.

Do your research before you buy your running shoes. Look at any pair of shoes you own. How do they wear? If they lean inward, in a v-shape, you are a pronator. The running shoes you purchase should provide extra support to the medial (inward) side. Knee pain may result if you do not train in anti-pronation shoes.

If you observe that your shoes wear in an outward pattern, you are a supinator. As you look at your shoes they are leaning away from one another. The type of running shoes you should purchase should be built up more to the outside, attempting to keep you on a level plane as you run. Excessively worn shoes on this lateral side may cause pain on the outside of your knees, and could also produce hip pain.

Heavier runners should avoid the feather-light shoes and go for more cushioned types.

If your foot is excessively narrow or excessively wide, check out brands that offer width-sizing.

Once you establish a brand and style to your liking, it is ok to order shoes online. But if you're a beginner, or have the desire to try a new style, it is essential to try a shoe on for size and fit, and it is a very good idea to take a 'test-drive,' by going for a short jog in the shoes before you make your purchase.

Just because your shoes don't appear to be worn out does not mean that the support life of the shoes hasn't expired. Consult your running log in order to keep track of the number of miles you have accumulated on your shoes. When the midsole of the shoe breaks down, your support is lost. You become defenseless, and the threat of injury increases dramatically. Take preventive measures. Have a new pair of shoes ready to go as soon as you feel the road encroaching on your feet. At the first sign of injury begin your rehabilitation with your shoes.

So you've changed shoes and your injury persists. What do you do next? Well, the old tried and true acronym 'RICE,' is still the best home remedy for curing injuries.

REST-Take a day off. It will do way more good than harm. Try alternative exercises, intense stretching, or just relax. Sometimes the body just needs a break. From an aerobic standpoint, three days off will not affect you at all. After that, the formula is: for each day off, it takes about two days to come back. Still, if a few days off is a means of avoiding a catastrophic injury, it is well worth it.

ICE-Next time you walk down a sidewalk, notice how the cement has a space between the blocks. This allows for expansion, for, as we learned in our high school science classes, heat causes expansion; while cold causes contraction. The cement needs room to expand during the hot, summer months. If your running injury has caused swelling, ice is the ideal therapy, as it reduces swelling. Many runners keep a Styrofoam cup in their freezers so they're ready to apply ice as needed. Ten minutes or so is sufficient, as too much ice may damage skin tissue and ultimately cause frostbite. After about a half hour, you may reapply ice. For sore muscles, many runners take ice baths. This runner is not one of those folks; as I would rather be water boarded than endure a cold water shock of any kind. Ice baths are, however, an excellent means of reducing swelled muscle tissue.

During the warmer months it is a good idea to use a simple garden hose as a method of therapy after a workout. In the early 1980s I had the opportunity to train with Rod Dixon, a New Zealander, who eventually went on to win the 1983 New York City Marathon. Dixon, who trained for a time in Reading, Pennsylvania, believed in this practice, and hosed down his legs after each workout. His philosophy was that this therapy works for race horses so it should work for us.

COMPRESSION-Wrapping an injured area, such as a hamstring, is a good idea. It works as a cast, and combined with an analgesic balm, can hasten the healing process.

ELEVATION-It's all about the blood flow, and not allowing the blood to pool is a quick way to recovery. From the hip down, when injured, keep legs elevated as much as possible.

I am a great believer in ibuprofen. It helps reduce swelling and keeps the blood flowing freely, so for my money, RICEI is a more appropriate acronym.

Podiatrists and chiropractors are valuable medical practitioners for runners. For the most part, they understand us and our obsessive need to return to our passion quickly and pain free.

My greatest chiropractic moment occurred in the fall of 2009. I am fortunate to enjoy the expertise of a terrific chiropractor. Jack Dolbin was a member of the Denver Broncos team that played in

Super Bowl XII in 1978. A native of Pottsville, he decided to return home and open a chiropractic practice after his NFL days were over. Jack is extremely knowledgeable, and obviously well versed in sports medicine. Although he cannot fully grasp the fanaticism of runners, he appreciates our healthy lifestyles and our training needs.

In July of 2009, my chronic lower back problem reared its ugly head again while, of all endeavors, I was picking weeds in the garden. A reach for that stubborn dandelion produced a stabbing pain that made me think I just got shanked. After a few days of rest, ice, and ibuprofen, I foolishly returned to training. During an easy seven-mile run on the Auburn trail with Brian Tonitis and his son, Matt, my right hamstring completely froze, locking, making it impossible to run another step. You've all experienced those excruciatingly painful hamstring cramps in the middle of the night. The kind that cause you to break out in a cold sweat and want to cry. Well, this was one of them. I had no choice but to enjoy a three-mile walk back to my car.

I had committed the classic runner's mistake. I came back too soon from an injury. In an unconscious manner, when we're injured, we fool ourselves into thinking we're completely healed when, in fact, we're not. In my case, the lower back muscle was still damaged and weak. I compensated for it by relying more heavily on my hamstring, thus straining it. What should have been four or five days off turned out to be several weeks of agonizing rest.

Doctor Dolbin took me in for therapy, and he was not alarmed. He assured me, if I followed his plan, I would be back on the road in a short period of time. He employed spinal manipulation, ultrasound, electrical stimulation of the hamstring, and presented me with a stretching regimen.

Using a sophisticated analytical procedure he measured me for a pair of orthotics. If you run long enough, you're probably going to need a pair of orthotics. They are custom-made to conform to your foot and to correct your foot imbalance. They are simply miraculous.

Years prior to this injury I had a set of these foot-levelers, which I had retired. This new set was lighter and more comfortable.

Having been unable to run a single step for several weeks, the orthotics were created and they fit perfectly. Doctor Dolbin checked them out, analyzed my foot plant and declared, "You can run tomorrow." I gave him a, "Yeah, right" look, but when I realized he was totally serious, I asked, "How far?" "A couple of miles" was his reply.

The results were spectacular. The day before, one running step caused a cramping in my hamstring. The next day, orthotics in place, I ran two miles, pain free.

The moral of the story: find a knowledgeable medical practitioner who you trust, stay with the person and heed their advice. My family doctor runs marathons, my podiatrist cycles, even my urologist is an avid tennis player. They have been the medical mechanics who have kept this fifty seven-year-old machine running to the point where my mileage has taken me around the world four times and can still crank out a sub three-hour marathon here and there. I am fortunate to have them on my team.

For runners, in addition to the word, 'injury,' the other hated 'I' word is: illness. Sickness really confounds runners. "I have a cold, congestion, a nagging cough, or the flu. What do I do? Should I run or should I take a few days off?"

There is no easy answer, although I have developed a philosophy over the years that has been fairly successful, and has cost minimal lost training time. If your illness lies below the neck, don't run. Above the neck, go out for an abbreviated workout.

Runners rely on our powerful twin engines: our lungs. Chest congestion impedes our lung function, and often by continuing to train we run the risk of further constricting our vital air passages. What begins as congestion may lead to bronchitis and possibly pneumonia. Besides, we have all tried to run through chest congestion and, for the most part, have failed. Airways, narrowed, cannot possibly deliver the oxygen needed for a quality running effort. It's like a clogged air filter on your car. Sit it out for a couple of days, then resume running when your engines have the oxygen they need to function efficiently.

Throughout my running career I have consistently maintained that, if I choose to take time off from the sport, it's going to be on my terms. Injuries and illness rob that option from us. As runners, our independent, self-reliant nature creates an obstinate attitude that is often counterproductive. Use good common sense when you're injured or ill. Don't be afraid to rely on the recuperative power of rest. Sleep, drink plenty of fluids, and consume the fruit and vegetable 'super foods.'

Few people have the ability to be close to nature and to "smell the roses" like we runners. When you're injured or ill, enjoy things from a different perspective. Take a walk, a bike ride, or a swim. If you're injured below the waist, go to the gym and pump some iron for your upper body strength. Bundle up under the covers, prop your legs up on a cozy sofa or chair. Relax and watch some mindless television. Read a good book. Attempt to put a positive spin on your affliction. When you return to training, you'll appreciate running more than ever.

MILE 13–WHY DO THEY HATE US SO MUCH?

We runners tend to have very healthy egos, but we all need to get over ourselves for a moment and accept a stark realization.

They hate us!

Oh, our family and friends, for the most part, still love us, but if you log your daily miles on the streets, highways, cities and villages of America, most of those folks who do not share your passion for running hate you.

It's an 'in your face' thing. If you're lifting weights in a gym, holed up somewhere running your miles on a treadmill, or hidden away in a park or a secluded trail, all is fine. You don't pose a threat to the largely out of shape, road-loving, drive-for-fifteen minutes to find a closer parking space at the local mall, public. When you amble down the road looking fit, you are taking road space away from Mr. Muscle Car. The ex-athlete who lost his fitness and gained fifty pounds now sees you, svelte and in shape, running past him. You are a grim reminder to him of what he was, or what he thinks he could be. Many older folks hate you, as they can't grasp the entire concept of what you're doing. In their time, hard physical work was the norm. People worked in factories, mines, shipyards and on farms. Few people were afforded the luxury of running miles on the roads after a difficult day performing a physically demanding job. To them we are freaks, who should be doing something more productive with our time.

They hate us because of the times we conduct our workouts. We're out there when they're out there.

It's safe to say that most of us are not independently wealthy. We perform our daily jobs, then wedge our workouts between our need to make a living and our family obligations. Many runners find it necessary to conduct their workout before they head off to work. So there you are, at 5:00 or 6:00 a.m. It's probably still dark. Most of those folks whose headlights blind you are on their way to miserable jobs that they detest. They're fumbling with their hot coffee, a jelly donut stuffed in their face. You're decked out in your reflective gear, looking fit, already having incinerated more calories in a half hour than they will burn in a day. They shake their heads, spill their coffee, and lay on the horn as they pass you.

Maybe you can squeeze in a run during your lunch break. Heading toward you is a carload of people who are ready to consume a massive lunch. The sight of you could actually inspire them to go the soup and sandwich route, but, in their mind, you're crazy. More frightening, however, are those who may decide to have a couple of martinis with their lunch. Those types are a downright danger to you. They laugh, joke about your stride, your outfit, or the shape of your body.

For most of us, though, our training begins when most people's work day ends, between 4:00 and 4:30 in the afternoon. For us, a daily run often serves as a stress release. The deadline you may not make, a confrontation with the boss, or a heated conversation with an irate customer are all a bit easier to deal with after you have put a couple of miles behind you.

But we're not like everyone else.

For many, that difficult work day ends with the additional stress of the daily commute. To the weary, stressed out driver, on the way home after a tough day, runners represent the ultimate manifestation of road rage. We become that nasty customer, as the frustrated store manager spots us cavorting down the street in front of him. We ARE the boss, as the disgruntled employee gnashes his teeth when he observes us chatting with each other, or laughing as we train. Often we are the dismal ending to a dismal day, and, to a large degree, the working public can't stand us.

As working folks ourselves, we often log our long training runs on weekends. Soccer moms and dads spill their lattes when they perceive we're in their way as they hurry to the match. Little League parents can't understand why we're not attending some game somewhere, with suntan lotion slathered on our faces, lamenting why our future major leaguer isn't the starting shortstop. They stare at our gaunt faces as they stuff theirs with french fries. We stand there exhausted after a fifteen-mile morning run, slugging down our replacement fluid drink.

Perhaps the most dangerous day of the week for runners, however, is Sunday. There you are striding down the street while legions of faithful are on their way to or from church. Over the years I have observed that people filled with the Lord are often the most vicious, refusing to yield an inch of precious road space, and sometimes even mouthing blasphemous epithets and obscene gestures at unsuspecting runners.

The irony of the public's hatred toward us is that we runners work hard at our jobs too; we take care of our families, attending games, meets, recitals, band concerts, and PTA meetings. We go to church, visit our elderly parents, take care of our household chores, AND we run.

During or after a snowstorm I inevitably encounter a red-faced snow shoveler, who leans on his shovel, stares at me curiously and states, "You should be doing this." For years I chuckled at the inane comment, but no more. I state the obvious and reply, "I've done it already!" Does snow magically disappear from your property when you're a runner?

Yes, we perform all the daily tasks our detractors perform, and we also run. We're the pretty girl that other pretty girls hate, simply because they're envious.

As their buttons pop at the belly, we all have heard our acquaintances proclaim, "You should eat more," or "You don't look good." Does being overweight equate with looking good?

A personal favorite of mine usually comes from someone who saw me on the road a few days ago. Their question is, "Are you still running?"

The pat on the belly and the "I'd be out there with you if it weren't for this," is a statement that I still have been unable to dignify with a proper response.

"I almost hit you the other day," draws from me this retort "Take a number!"

Recently, an eighty-something driver instructed us to, "Get off the road." Clearly the road is his exclusive, personal domain.

We've all heard the military hoot of "Hut two, three, four," as a verbal manifestation of people's disdain as well as an attempt at humor.

There's the occasional instructive driver who studies his speedometer and informs you that you're going seven miles an hour.

Many of us have been pelted with snowballs, squirted with water guns, grazed by cars, and harassed by little kids.

On vacation in Punta Cana, Dominican Republic last summer I received international scorn when a German mother and daughter actually laughed hysterically as I ran by.

The middle finger has been thrust at us thousands of times. "Get the f— off the road" is a favorite mantra, as are the mouth gestures that include f-bombs and virtually every other derogatory term known to man.

For male runners, who especially threaten the macho American he-man, skinny guys in shorts can only mean one thing. "Faggot" is an insult that has been hurled at us on numerous occasions.

Randy Haas and I once received the ultimate manifestation of "runner rage." As we ambled along the side of the street in a local community, we observed the police car speed by us. Naturally we suspected there had been some type of local emergency. We had no idea the source of local lawbreaking happened to be we. The officer, who served as the local police chief, hung a U-turn, Starsky and Hutch style, in the parking lot of a local grocery store, and headed back toward us. Drawing within several yards, he positioned the vehicle in a manner that blocked our potential escape route. Half expecting to be wrestled to the ground and cuffed, we came to a screeching halt. The chief exited the vehicle and approached. He warned us, in no uncertain terms, that there was a town ordinance prohibiting runners from running on the street when a sidewalk was available. That's right, a law against running. My response was, "You've got to be kidding." He assured me he wasn't kidding, let us off with a warning, and we were on our way. Needless to say, after a brief stint on a cracked, dangerous sidewalk we returned to the road. Apparently the long arm of the law was having a bad day so why not take it out on the easily visible moving targets.

There is an estimated more than 36 million runners in the United States, so we can fight back against the haters. In subtle conversation, do not be ashamed of the fact that you run, rather, embrace it. If the guy pats his gut and tells you that's why he can't run with you, tell him to run a few miles, lose the gut, then he CAN go with you. Maybe you can advise those who "Almost hit you," that you have a really good attorney who would enjoy acquiring compensation from them after they DO hit you. Inform the person at the cocktail party who is interested as to whether or not you're still running, that he or she will be the first to know when you decide to retire from the sport.

Get the license plate of the car after the driver whips you the middle finger. Yell at the little kid who insults you or stop at his house for a talk with mom or dad.

In your community, lobby for that bike or walking path. If you already have one, go to a meeting and make sure the trail is properly maintained. Keep in mind that, in most states, pedestrians possess the right of way. Drivers do not have exclusive rights to the road. Unless prohibited, as in the case of Interstate Highways, runners have every right to safely occupy their share of the road.

Sometimes the non running public needs a stern wake up call. Last year, Eric Anchorstar approached the twenty five-mile mark of a local marathon, tired and exhausted. It just wasn't his day. He knew he was far off his projected time, his legs ached, and his goal had been reduced to simply finishing the race. The crowds swelled in the college town as the finish line neared. Off to his left Eric spotted a college student, a race spectator, mockingly drawing up next to him. The young man wore baggy shorts, a concert T-shirt, and had a cigarette hanging from his mouth, which he puffed, blowing the smoke in the direction of the runners. He strode along, next to the group of runners, raising his legs high, like a drum major. Anchorstar, enraged, looked to his right, asking a fellow competitor, "How much will you give me if I deck this guy?" The gentleman jokingly replied, "Fifty bucks." Without breaking stride, Anchorstar, who possesses a large bicep, adorned with a Boston Marathon tattoo, nurtured by years of weightlifting, delivered a swift forearm shiver to the student's sternum, knocking him to the ground, cigarette flying. Runners around him cheered, the crowd was stunned, and the wounded student could only mutter, "Asshole!"

When recounting the event Anchorstar observed, "What he did was an insult to every runner in that race, from the 2:20 marathoner to the six-hour marathoner. I just couldn't stand for that."

Most of us aren't preachers, nor are we running gurus. We enjoy what we do. If others choose to pursue fitness through running, we support and embrace their efforts. For the most part, we do not tell people to run, but we should be afforded the respect to do what we do without harassment.

It will never happen.

Throughout the country running has become more mainstream, but haters still abound. They hate us out of jealousy. They hate us because they may see in us something they want to be or something they once were. They hate us because, by our visibility, we threaten them. They hate us because we are able to manage our time, doing all the things they do and more. They hate us because every day, in their faces, they see men and women of all ages, many who don't necessarily 'look' like runners, on the roads, in all types of weather, enjoying themselves, and staying fit. They hate us because we're somewhat obsessive-compulsive. We enjoy competition, even if the competition is us; running farther, faster, beating last year's mileage and times.

So don't take it personally.

For every hater there's an admirer. Someone who respects what we do. You all have your admirers. That person who has been inspired by you, who has asked you how to get started with a running program. The one you encouraged to enter a race. The coworker who, thanks to your training advice, has lost ten pounds.

This sport is more than you. It is those you touch, not only by your words, but by your example. Each one of those folks you have positively impacted negates a thousand detractors.

A car passes, lays on his horn, flashes me a fist as a gesture of his affection. My response is to smile and wave.

Each time we get out there on the roads we wave away our detractors. We leave our footprints. We complete our workouts. We defeat the haters.

MILE 14–THE DIET BOOK

I hope you are enjoying this book, because I'm happy to announce that I've completed my next work. It will be a diet book. After all, it seems as though everywhere one turns these days there's a new diet book on the shelves. By reading these pages, you're the recipient of a two for one deal. You have the opportunity to read my next book now.

So, here it is: my book.

First, of course, I'll thank all who inspired me. Then I'll print the Table of Contents.

What is the name of the book?

"Eat less. Exercise more."

The entire content of the book?

Eat less. Exercise more.

The End.

Ok, maybe there should be more to it than that, but when one examines the ridiculous methods of weight loss, and the subsequent written accounts of their success, some common sense needs to be applied to the topic.

Over the years there have been hundreds of devices, theories, and food, or lack of food solutions to the battle of the bulge.

There's the starvation diet. Eat a couple of grapefruits a day and you're good to go. Go without carbohydrates forever and you'll lose weight. Try nuts. Eat lots of carbohydrates. Never eat animal byproducts. Eat more protein. Try the Ab Dominizer, the Leg Cruncher, the Butt Blaster. Wear a rubber suit. Create a concoction made of pineapple juice and you'll shed pounds. Just drink liquids. A shot of some kind of vitamin here or there might do the trick. Or, and if all else fails, get yourself stapled, have a big old rubber band inserted in your abdomen and simply choke that food out of your stomach.

If all these bizarre methods don't work for you, perhaps you should buy the book featuring a cover with the Mr. Twelve Pack Abs, shirtless Adonis; or the one with the bikini-clad Goddess. Give it a catchy title like, "The North Shore Diet," "The Sierra Nevada Diet," "The Las Vegas Weight Loss Manual," or the "Santa Barbara Seafood Plan," and many Americans, obsessed with losing weight without any effort, will run right out and snatch it off the shelf.

My book idea is a leaner version of these fluffy, money making missives. Granted, maybe I could get some celebrity to promote it. Clearly, most of these self-absorbed Hollywood types use all sorts of 'natural' methods of looking fit. For example, Botox is natural, isn't it? So are those numerous surgeries and tucks. By the time they're done with all of their cuts and tucks they look like emaciated burn victims.

Let's face it. It's really not that complicated. And, as a nation, Americans better lose weight soon, because we're killing ourselves.

We are the fattest nation on the planet. Hell, we are the fattest nation in the history of the planet.

The statistics are astounding.

A body mass index of 18.5 to 25 is considered to be a healthy weight. 'Overweight' is defined as BMI of more than 25 to 30. 'Obese' is a BMI over 30; while 'Extremely Obese' is a BMI more than 40. If one is extremely obese, nearly half of their body is composed of fat! Mercifully, only about 6% of our population falls into this category.

Over two-thirds of the adults in the United States are overweight or obese, according to data from the National Health and Nutrition Examination Survey (NHANES) 2003–2006 and 2007–2008.

The same survey reveals that 12.4 percent of children between the ages of two to five and 17 percent of children ages six to eleven are overweight. About 17.6 percent of adolescents (age twelve to nineteen) are overweight, and the statistics appear to be rising.

People who are obese are much more likely to die of a plethora of diseases, as opposed to folks who maintain a healthy weight level. Cardiovascular disease, cancer, Type 2 diabetes, and fatty liver disease are all on the rise, and obesity is the main culprit.

It's costly to be fat. On average, people who are considered obese pay $1,429 (42 percent) more in health care costs than normal-weight individuals.

Statistics compiled by NHANES indicate that only 31 percent of U.S. adults report that they engage in regular leisure-time physical activity (defined as either three sessions per week of vigorous physical activity lasting twenty minutes or more or five sessions per week of light-to-moderate physical activity lasting thirty minutes or more). About forty percent of adults report no leisure-time physical activity.

So, back to my diet book.

These statistics are alarming, but they are so easy to reverse. There is no magic formula, pill, or machine. Shedding pounds is easy, cheap, and attainable for anyone.

First, eat less.

One need not become a vegan. Half of the formula to weight loss is, quite simply, to consume less food.

Pass up a snack.

Resist that extra helping.

If the label indicates the product contains a high percentage of fat, don't buy it.

Moderation is the key. Eat a steak tonight, but don't eat a steak five nights a week. Treat yourself to a Big Mac once in a while, but don't eat one once a week.

Cut down on your portions. Americans still think that bigger is better. It's ok for a plate not to be overflowing with food.

Throw away the salt shaker. We get enough salt in our preserved foods to fill some small seas. Eat real food, not products.

All that stuff that looks the same as when it grows in the ground, when it hangs on vines, or on trees, it's all good for you. The crunch of an apple, the burst of sweetness as the orange slice meets your tongue, antioxidant-rich blueberries or potassium-filled bananas beat a bag of potato chips any day.

And, yes, breakfast is a very important meal. Try cereal and some fresh fruit rather than a donut.

Eat broccoli until you fart. Eat asparagus until you smell its pungent odor when you pee.

We all like to look at colors. We'll all be healthier if we eat more of them.

Start a garden. Tomatoes can be planted just about anywhere. Few endeavors are more satisfying than growing vegetables and harvesting them.

A dietician I'm not. Common sense simply should dictate. Eat less. But eat more good stuff. When you do, you'll be halfway there.

Then, exercise more.

Ordinary folks, every day, all over this country, keep in shape by doing very ordinary things.

Most mornings, on my way to work, I see Dr. Leslie Dubowitz.

A renowned local physician, Dr. Dubowitz rarely misses a day of exercise. In his sixties, he walks several miles, and he is undeterred by weather. He's as addicted as any runner I know. His pace is steady. His dedication is remarkable.

My father died at the age of eighty-eight. Fifty years earlier, at age thirty-eight, he suffered a heart attack. For most of those fifty years, my mother made it her mission to keep him alive. She did a very good job. My mother never cooked fried food, never used salt, and cooked a variety of food in moderation. Fruits and vegetables were always plentiful in my home. Potato chips were not.

Until my father was eighty-five years of age, he and my mother would walk from their home to the western end of Pottsville. My dad wore a pedometer attached to his belt. He was proud to boast that the distance of his workout was 2.1 miles. They followed the out and back route three days a week, at a brisk pace. Two tiny individuals, with little body fat, arm in arm, waving and greeting neighbors and friends along the way. My mother is now ninety years old and suffers from macular degeneration. She possesses only 10% of her vision. In addition, her walking days are over thanks to severe osteoporosis. Still, she refuses to become sedentary. Each day she reports to me that she "takes her exercises." For a half hour, she lifts her two and a half pound hand weights. When I assist her by grabbing her around the arm, I can feel the taut biceps that are the size and consistency of tangerines.

My dad's childhood friend, Ed 'Kid Lightning' Tonitis, rarely missed his daily walk through the streets of Palo Alto.

Palo Alto is a flat town, southeast of Pottsville that stretches about a mile and a quarter from bridge to bridge. In his eighties, Ed Tonitis, Brian's father, would take his daily walk, often encountering his son and I on our training runs. His greeting was always the same. "Pick em up and put em down."

Getting one's heart rate up above 100 beats a minute for twenty minutes, three to four times a week, is the minimum to maintain a healthy body.

That's only one hour a week.

How you do it doesn't matter. Walking, running, biking, swimming, hiking, rollerblading, weightlifting, or any means necessary to elevate your heart rate is great.

Ever notice how you don't feel like eating after you've completed a workout?

How about when you're sitting around watching television or spending hours on a computer or a video game?

My goodness, you're famished from working those fingers so hard!

A runner melts approximately one-hundred calories for each mile run. Remember, the heart is a muscle, the body's most important muscle. It needs work in order to remain strong. Flex it whenever you can.

Well, I guess I embellished my book a little more than I had planned.

We live in a magnificent age. Everything is, literally, at our fingertips. Our modern inventions have enabled us to limit our physical activity in the course of our every day life.

Few of us are required to bale the hay or plow the field. Jobs that require manual labor are performed by fewer people. Young people today have no idea that a television set could exist without a remote.

Eating less and exercising more is not only a formula for a longer life. It is a recipe for a healthier life. Those who practice this advice tend to not only extend their lives, but are able to compete and enjoy physical activities well into their eighties and beyond.

Until it's proven differently, we really do only go around once, and it is our choice whether we want our body to be a cathedral or a shack.

The formula contained in my diet book may be a simple one, but it's not always easy to follow. Fatigue, muscle soreness, and occasional injuries sometimes cause us to question why we engage in aerobic activities when most of the population seems to be fat and happy.

On a recent visit to my family doctor I asked, "Do obese people feel as bad as I do the day after I run a race or complete a hard workout?"

His answer was priceless.

"Joe, you feel bad a day or two after a race. I suspect obese people feel bad EVERY day."

Eat less, exercise more and your good days will far outnumber your bad days.

MILE 15–EXCUSES, EXCUSES

Let's talk about two very different types of people who use the crutch of excuse-making in different ways.

When you choose to become a runner, it sometimes seems as though you have opened a door from which excuses have resided and have now chosen to come out and manifest themselves. The plethora of the excuses ranges from the ridiculous to, well, the more ridiculous.

Most runners have been subjected to the person who, at one time, in their mind, was a tremendous runner. Today, however, that ex-phenom is much too busy or way too fat to participate in the sport. The former excuse is a slap in the face to us, as runners. Are you saying that we are NOT as busy as you, or, in the case of the latter excuse, that we might look like you if we chose not to pursue a healthy lifestyle?

Several years ago I had my car serviced at a garage, located seven miles from my home. I dropped the car off in the morning and ran back to my residence. In the afternoon, when the repairs had been completed, I ran back to pick up the car. A fifty-something year-old gentleman sat two feet behind the desk, his belly nearly touching it. He asked me if I had run to down to pick up the car and I responded affirmatively. He proceeded to pat his ample gut and tell me how he had run a four-something minute mile in high school. He finished his praise of his former self by proclaiming he now possessed a "good body gone bad."

Perceived ailments or former injuries are grade-A excuses. "I'd run but my knees are bad." Perhaps the extra hundred pounds you're toting around contributes to your knee problem more than a mile or two here or there?

Hips, back, and feet may also be added to this very formidable list, and all are exacerbated by increased weight and a sedentary lifestyle.

Don't get me wrong, a back injury or knee injuries can end one's running career, but all of us have heard our share of bogus injury excuses.

One of the best excuses is one I wish I had a dollar for every time it's hurled at me. Actually it's an admonition and an excuse all wrapped in one. "You're going to ruin your knees." Or, "when you're in your seventies, you're going to be crippled." While none of us are certain what the Golden Years has in store for us, recent studies have indicated that, as boomers are aging, they are actually experiencing fewer arthritis symptoms than non runners.

A study conducted by the Fifty Plus Runners Association and published in *Arthritis Research & Therapy,* under the title "Aerobic Exercise and its Impact on Musculoskeletal Pain in Older Adults: a fourteen-Year Prospective, Longitudinal Study," compared runners who run about twenty six-miles a week to runners who averaged around two miles a week The study concluded that runners in the former group experienced "about twenty-five percent less musculoskeletal pain" then the two mile a week group.

Strong muscles support joints better than weak ones. Indeed, obesity contributes more to arthritis than accumulated miles over a lifetime.

There's the "I don't want to get too skinny" excuse. Ok, a running program is controlled by no one other than the individual who is doing the running. Losing TOO much weight? Uh, don't run as much! How about, "I get bored when I run." Personally, I believe the words, "bored," and "boring," are way too prevalent on our society. Is a little boredom better than coronary bypass surgery? Isn't boring preferable to Type II diabetes? Are video games boring? What about reality television?

"I don't like to sweat" is a favorite of mine. Like most of you, I live in an area where we actually have a summer. I'm not really sure what the folks who don't like to sweat do during the months of June, July, and August.

"I'm more of a sprinter; I could never run long distances." Your experience may be different from mine, but most of the folks who label themselves as "sprinters," leave Usain Bolt, the Jamaican 100-meter world-record holder and Olympic champion, with little to fear. Besides, if one indeed does have a sprinter's background, he or she is already a runner, complete with competitive instincts. It is not too difficult to morph from a being sprinter to a distance runner.

Excuses, however, are not limited to those who feel compelled to offer alibis for why they don't run.

Sooner or later, if you've run long enough, you will be consumed by a gnawing desire to enter a race. You may choose a small local race, an event that may attract one-hundred to two-hundred participants. Perhaps you will run a race for a local charity, or maybe you'll attempt a major race, the kind that draws thousands of runners.

No matter which type of race you choose or what type of pace you run, whether you are old or young, whether you are serious about your racing or not, all race participants will eventually come to realize one undeniable fact: runners are full of excuses.

Racing is a strange phenomenon. Many runners take racing very seriously. They are there to win, either overall, or in their age division. Others enter races for a variety of reasons. Some folks see racing as a means of conducting a speed workout. Still others figure they will always run faster in a race, surrounded by other runners, than they will in a training run. For some, racing is a social event.

At every level, though, before, after, and, sometimes even during the race, a sea of excuses lies there ready to drown many race competitors.

Here are some of my favorites.

"I was just running this race as a workout."

Ok, maybe it's me, but, for the past thirty-five years I still cannot figure out why someone would use a race as a workout. I use a workout as a workout. I really don't feel the need to pay a fee, pick up another T-shirt, or earn another trophy or medal. If you're going to train, then train. But if I beat you in a race, dammit, I've beaten you. If you have been foolish enough to put your talent and reputation on the line for a workout, then accept the fact that you've been defeated. Don't soften your blow or dampen my victory over you with a lame excuse about running a workout.

"Oh, man, I was out partying until (insert time) last night."

Well, in the words of Forrest Gump's mom, "Stupid is as stupid does." Is there really anything so stupid? Racing is an intense, difficult endeavor. Why would anyone want to exponentially increase that difficulty with the effects of alcohol and a lack of sleep? The late

New York Yankees slugger, Mickey Mantle admittedly showed up for games after evenings of hard drinking, but he had the luxury of resting in the dugout between innings. There are no innings in a race. Besides humiliating yourself with a sub-par performance, there is a real physical danger, as alcohol dehydrates the human body. Racing with a hangover in a hot summer day is a very bad idea.

When we select a race, we enter the event with the knowledge that there is a very good chance we'll be nicked up on race day. Sore muscles, a bruised heel, or an inflamed tendon, are all injuries we can race through successfully and have no place on the excuse menu. However, finishing behind you, many adversaries will present a laundry list of injuries for your consideration. Implicit, of course, is that if they were uninjured you'd have never had a chance.

Most of us have a fairly good grasp on mathematical distance, but some runners don't. Races are, of course, set at proscribed distances. One's time is based on completing that particular distance. When that distance is covered more quickly by 'Runner A,' over 'Runner B,' Runner A is the winner. Pretty straight forward, right? Hmmm . . . not so fast.

At the awards ceremony of my last 10K race, a runner, the guy who finished behind me in the age group, proclaimed, "I was catching up to you in the last mile."

Exactly what does that mean? The race distance was 6.2 miles, not 6.4 miles. Additionally, how does he know he was catching up to me. Maybe I was enjoying the scenery. Possibly I would have found another gear and increased my lead over him had I known he was, "catching up to me." It seems as though, if a competitor finishes behind you, the race distance is just never long enough.

Some marathoners are seriously mathematically challenged. One local marathoner, who never broke the 2:25 barrier, could simply not accept the fact that I was able to consistently defeat him at that distance, while he dominated me in shorter events, would always remind me that he was on a sub-2:20 pace at the twenty-mile mark. Sadly, for this master excuse-maker, the marathon distance is 26.2 miles.

Weather is another popular excuse. If you run enough races, those who are left in your wake will let you know how poorly they run in the heat, the cold, in the wind, in high humidity, low humidity,.... you get the picture.

Excuse makers are sometimes their own worst enemies. Prior to the race they often brag about their killer workouts and often set unrealistic goals. At the end of the race, when they have failed to reach their stated goal, they feel compelled to explain to you their contrived reasons for failure.

These folks are not bad people. They are somewhat delusional, and, for the most part they are compensating with their mouths what they lack in training or ability.

Race when you feel you are running your best. Respect your fellow runners. Excuses are a sign of disrespect for those who are engaging in the same difficult endeavor as you. If you are injured or ill on race day, either stay home or accept your fate with honor. Most runners respect a vanquished fellow competitor who offers the compliment, "You ran a great race today."

To an honest, honorable competitor, when it comes to race day excuses, there are no excuses. Only your feet should do the talking.

MILE 16–FRUSTRATION . . . FULFILLMENT

Early May can still be a fickle time for weather in the coal region of northeastern Pennsylvania.

At the Silver Bowl, a stadium located in the football-crazed town of Mount Carmel, tucked among the mountains of coal that was, at one time, the lifeblood of the region, the crisp May air nipped at the spectators producing a plethora of jackets and sweatshirts, and perfect conditions for distance runners.

Local high schools' athletes had gathered for the 2005 Schuylkill All-League Meet, the championship event for schools in the Schuylkill Track and Field League. Top finishers in the events would move onto the District Meet the following week, where the elite finishers would, by virtue of their place or time, qualify for the Pennsylvania State Championships, held on the last weekend in May.

Although I had competed in more than 400 races in my running career, my nerves began to get the best of me as the start of the race neared. This, however, was not my race. It was my daughter, Megan, fifteen, who stretched and jogged in the paddock area, as she warmed up for the upcoming 800-meter competition.

Just as every parent wants their child to have a better life than they did, almost every athlete who has tasted competition has aspirations of greatness for one's child, whether it is in the sport of the parent, or another sport.

Distance runners are different though. We're not like Al Bundy. Al, star of the popular hit television series of the '80s and 90s, "Married With Children," would fondly recall the bygone days of his high school football career when he set the Polk High School record of scoring four touchdowns in one game. Sadly, Al's days of glory were far in the rear view mirror. Distance runners, though, are often still competing in their middle ages, so when we attempt to guide our children, it is not from the perspective of a long gone sports career. We are not swilling our drinks, laying our beer bellies on the table and proclaiming, "back when I played . . . ," rather we are still, very much, in the competitive mix. That can be both a blessing and a curse.

Megan, my youngest daughter, began her running career in a race near Disney World, in 1992. She was two years old. We were on vacation, and prior to a 10K event for which I was registered, the race organizers conducted a kid's fifty-yard dash for toddlers under the age of three. She won.

During her grade school years, Megan took a keen interest in all sports, possibly fueled by my fanatical passion for the Philadelphia Eagles, Phillies, and 76ers. She also had a dynamic 4th grade teacher, Jack Spleen, who motivated his students to write by having them correspond with prominent sports figures.

Although she played basketball, softball, soccer, and danced, it was in the area of running in which she excelled.

Throughout my running career I witnessed numerous runners who imposed their adult training philosophy on their young children. Eight and Nine-year-olds were participating in 5K and sometimes even 10K events. It's like the baseball parent who has his child throw and throw, until he injures his arm, or just downright hates the sport. I was determined not to be that type of parent. Megan trained during her early years for two specific events. The first is a very fine national program, sponsored by Hershey Foods, called the Hershey Track and Field Program. Youngsters compete in age-group running, jumping, and field events. On the track, races from the 50-meter dash to the 1600 meter run are contested. My daughter attended the state championship meet on three occasions, winning the state championship in the 800 meters at the age of fourteen.

Her other event on which she annually focused was a local mile street race, held each Memorial Day. She consistently won her age group in the race.

Megan ran many races, but never trained more than two miles in a workout until she reached high school. As a freshman, she had a good cross country season, but her true love was track, where she competed in the 800 and 1600-meter races. She battled some injuries during her freshman seasons, but managed to do well, despite training that still involved very few miles and not too much hard work.

During her sophomore year she made it to States in cross country and lost only one 800-meter race during her track and field season. A tall, strong runner from Shamokin Area, a school to the north of us, used her strength to defeat my daughter handily on Megan's home track during a regular season meet.

The gun sounded and the field of 16 runners took off. The women's 800-Meter event at Leagues had begun. Megan positioned herself well, remaining near the front of the pack and out of traffic. As the competitors completed the first lap, it became a two-person race. The

Shamokin runner held the lead, but Megan paced herself two strides behind, looking very strong. Down the backstretch, with the crowd cheering, Megan made her move. Long, thin legs churning, ponytail flopping in the still air, she surged, passing her opponent, continuing to apply the pressure for another twenty meters. Around the penultimate turn, she held on, galloping to the roar of the crowd as she strode down the final straightaway. She broke the tape in two minutes, 27.2 seconds, and she was the League Champion. From my vantage point near the finish line, hoarse from cheering, she leaped into my arms. I was one of my proudest moments.

A week later, at the district meet, she ran a 2:23.6, barely missing an opportunity to go to the state meet. As a sophomore, she was at the top of her game.

It was downhill from there.

As a junior her times ballooned. At cross country meets she was a shell of her former self, struggling, straining on the hills she used to own. Track season was even worse. Just a year after her stellar performance at the League Meet, she placed far back in the pack, no longer a factor. No longer a Phenom.

By the time Megan became a high school senior, I was no longer able to attend her meets. Her League

Championship days were so far behind her, and she was no longer the top runner on her own squad. Minor injuries plagued her. Social activities became more important to her. She became a child of divorce.

Throughout her decline I observed that, for a high school runner, reasons for failure are minimal. A debilitating injury can derail a career. Poor coaching may have an impact, but 90% of the time it comes down to lack of motivation. No one can make a person want to run. Megan simply lost her desire. She trained woefully little, and it caught up to her. As a distance runner, there is absolutely no shortcut to success. A shortcut simply does not exist. In events from the 800 meters and beyond, one must put in the miles, and do the proper speed work. It's like any other recipe. You add the ingredients and observe the finished product.

I blamed myself. I failed her. I was devastated. I have been around the sport for more than three decades and coached countless runners, both as a team coach as well as an individual coach. For months, I wallowed in self-pity, wondering what could have been, obsessing over what I had done wrong Once I dreamed of running a marathon with my daughter. Now I realized that the dream was shattered.

I was wrong.

My oldest daughter, Kelly, may qualify as the perfect child. Now thirty-three, she is a social studies teacher in the Eastern York School District in southern Pennsylvania.

Kelly has never known the meaning of the word 'trouble,' because she has never put herself in a position to get into trouble. She was an excellent student in high school, and, although painfully shy at the time, fell in love with the University of South Carolina when I took her there on a visit. She moved to the campus, some nine hours from her home, had a stellar academic career, worked for a state senator, and earned her Bachelor's Degree in three years. In another year she earned her Master's Degree from South Carolina.

Kelly, however, had no interest in any sport of any kind. She accepted my running addiction, but never quite understood it. Very passive, she had a difficult time grasping my competitive nature.

So, I was more than mildly shocked in November 2009 when she called to announce, "Dad, I'm gonna run a marathon." Her previous running experience: zero. She had never run a race. In fact she had never logged a single training mile. Her goal: the San Diego marathon, some seven months later.

Kelly became inspired after she attended a meeting sponsored by Team in Training, a fund raising arm of the Leukemia/Lymphoma Society. For her part, she would be required to raise a specified amount of money for the charity. Team in Training would sponsor her trip to San Diego, but more importantly, experienced, coaches would guide her through her training.

Needless to say, however, I remained apprehensive. I thought she should start with the half marathon distance. The marathon is a major challenge for the most experienced runners.

She emailed the program to me and it was very sound. She would build her mileage with a long run each weekend. A few weeks before the marathon she would complete a twenty-mile training run.

Through a great deal of hard work she was able to raise the funds. She held bake sales, sold candy bars, and even bought a cuddly rabbit to use as a fund raiser for children to have their picture taken with a 'real' Easter Bunny. Thanks to incredible dedication and extraordinary coaching and support from her fellow runners, she felt prepared to take on the marathon distance.

On a warm, sunny June day in San Diego, she completed a seven-month journey that began from no miles a week, ending with a completed marathon to her credit, with a time of six hours, 29 minutes.

This sport does, indeed, have strange addictive qualities, and my daughter became an addict. She ran several short local races, a nine-mile leg of the Baltimore Marathon Relay, and decided to run the 2010 Philadelphia Marathon in November.

My daughter and I WOULD be running a marathon together.

We did.

I finished in 2:58:56, then waited for Kelly. As she rounded the final curve, tears filled my eyes. I was overcome with emotion. In her second marathon, she had shaved one hour off her time, running 5:29:35. It was one year, to the day, since she began her life as a long distance runner. She has more marathons planned for the future, and at this writing we are both registered for the 2011 Philadelphia Marathon, where she hopes to shatter the five-hour mark.

Running is the most individual of all individual sports. When one makes a commitment to succeed as a runner, success is usually imminent. Preaching, cajoling, bribing, threatening, or any other means of persuasion will not inspire a runner to put forth an effort if the desire is not present.

The life of a distance runner is never-ending journey. There are always faster runners out there. They key to success is to be the best trained runner. In distance running, as in life, preparation is essential. It starts with reasonable goals. When I was thirty, I ran my best marathon in a time of 2:22:54. Now, in my late fifties I know those days are long gone. My goals have changed. I strive to defeat runners in my age group. It is fun, though, to beat people half my age. Today I still train as hard as my body allows. No one is telling me to do it. It is a personal decision all runners must make.

As parents we seek to guide our children. It is a tightrope we walk. On one hand, we want them to succeed. If they play the violin, they must practice for endless hours. If they are competitive runners, they must run. As I look back at my daughters and their running careers, I regret that Megan did not realize her potential, but I have quit blaming myself. The decision was hers. She is a good person with a kind heart. She will succeed in the race of life. Running competitively was not a priority for her at that time in her life.

At this writing Megan is training for a 5K race. Kelly is training for a half marathon. I can see the three of us running a race together soon.

That's fulfillment.

Kelly Muldowney
Philadelphia Marathon 2010

MILE 17–GREAT RACES

If I were to win the Powerball jackpot, one of the things I would do, if I ever gathered the motivation to leave my hammock and my Caribbean Island retreat, would be to travel the world, running great road races, big and small.

In this chapter I will provide a sampling of my favorite races, at varying race distances, within an hour or two from my home. In a large sense, I have run more than 400 races in my career, from Toronto to Bermuda, but most have been located in my small corner of the world. Undoubtedly, you have many quality races near where you reside. Maybe you have run some of the same races you'll read about in the next few pages, or maybe you'd like to. If not, I'm certain some of the same criteria I use to rate my races will match yours.

Reading, Pennsylvania has always been known for its great races. Throughout my career I have run everything from a 24-hour relay to the steeplechase, a race distance of approximately two-miles, in which runners jump hurdles and slog through a water trough, in and around the Reading area.

These days, a company called Pretzel City Sports conducts a number of unique events throughout the year that attract thousands of participants. They stage mud races, trail runs, twelve-hour relays, as well as duathlons, (run and cycle races), and triathlons (running, cycling, and swimming).

From May to September, Pretzel City Sports conducts a series of 'Thirsty Thursday" 5K events. The races are held in the evenings, on the third Thursday of the month, and are staged at a local Irish pub. Advertised as "no frills" races, they attract three-hundred to four-hundred runners, who enjoy the flat, fast gravel trail course that follows the Schuylkill River, as well as the food and refreshments, which include a free beer, available at the end of the race.

The number of 5K races has increased more rapidly than the national debt. It's easy to find a race, but difficult to find a good one. If you're looking for a well-organized, low key event, that combines a fast course with a party atmosphere, the Thirsty Thursday 5K race series is an excellent choice.

Successful local races offer something for everybody. Few races accomplish this objective more successfully than the Tom Ausherman Memorial Five-Mile Run. Celebrating its 24th year in 2011, the race honors the patriarch of the Ausherman family, who tragically passed away at the finish line of a local race in 1987. Tom Ausherman was one of the founders of the Chambersburg Road Runners Club, and was also a Marine Corps veteran, who was named the Marine of the Year in Pennsylvania in 1983. The local Marine Corps League, the Tom Ausherman Memorial Committee, and the Chambersburg Road runners conduct the event each August.

The Ausherman race has grown to attract nearly four hundred runners annually to the quaint town of Chambersburg, nestled in the lush green farm country of south central Pennsylvania.

Runners of all abilities enjoy this race for several reasons, not the least of which is the fast course. The USA Track and field-certified course has produced some incredibly fast times, including astounding course records of 22 minutes, 43 seconds, set by Kenyan Reuben Cheb II, in 2004 for the men; and the female record of 26:04, set by Zivile Bilcivnrite, from the Ukraine, in 2003.

Superb course management, accurate splits at each mile, and an out and back course that tends to lean downhill during the latter half of the race add to the lure of the event.

Like many races these days, the Ausherman Five-Miler, cognizant that many veteran runners possess drawers full of cotton T-shirts, offers dry wicking T-shirts to its participants.

For the elite runners, more than $2600 in prize money is offered, but the real depth of the awards lies in the thirty-one age divisions for men and women, ranging from under twelve to over eighty. Marines are also honored with five awards in their own division, and the first place male and female high school runner receives the Tim Cook Memorial Award, presented in honor of Chambersburg's revered cross country coach who, along with his wife, was killed in a tragic automobile accident in 2002.

Trophies and medals are often coveted mementos of our youth, but as we age and compete more frequently, we appreciate unique reminders of races well run. The Ausherman race offers hand hewn pottery to all award winners. The crocks are suitable for a trophy case or as home ornaments.

The post-race party is magnificent. There is plenty of water, soda and beer. Sandwiches, snacks, and delicious slices of pie are served at the Marine Corps League.

Finally, whether you are among the elite, or near the rear of the pack, the Ausherman race holds your interest to the very end, because, each finisher is entered into a random drawing for a trip to the Bermuda Marathon. And if the beautiful island isn't for you, you may take the cash instead.

This race is best known for the hospitality of the folks of Chambersburg, and, particularly the Ausherman family. Tim and John Ausherman, veteran runners, have fine tuned the race each year, accommodating the needs of the racers. The entire Ausherman extended family plans and executes the race. Their father, for whom the race is dedicated, would be proud of their efforts.

Wedged between the rolling hills of north-central Pennsylvania and the sleepy Susquehanna River lies the small town of Berwick. To most residents of this region of Pennsylvania the mention of Berwick evokes images of hard-nosed high school football. Indeed, led by legendary, now retired coach George Curry, the Berwick Bulldogs have won six state high school football titles. Although long distance running plays second fiddle to the pigskin in the town, Berwick, Pennsylvania is the home to one of the oldest and most prestigious races in the country, and, indeed, boasts a vibrant running community featuring several unique races throughout the year.

Berwick's Run for the Diamonds is held annually on Thanksgiving Day, beginning on Market Street, in downtown Berwick. What's more, in this community of hardworking individuals, this race, the epitome of hard work and dedication, has been contested since 1908, when thirteen runners lined up to tackle the challenge. Officially, the first women to compete in this event toed the line in 1972, when two women crossed the finish line. It was cancelled twice, during World War I, and in 2009 celebrated its 100th anniversary. A record field of 1,985 runners completed the centennial race. The race is a favorite among Canadians, who have maintained a presence at the event since the inaugural run.

More than thirty Olympians, including Boston Marathon icon, Johnny Kelley, have run this race in its over one-hundred-year history. Two-time U.S. Olympian Pete Pfitzinger holds the course record, an astounding 43 minutes, 21 seconds, set in 1980. He was closely followed by former U.S. 10K record holder, Greg Fredericks, who blazed a 43:41 in placing second that year.

The Run for Diamonds was formerly called the "Berwick Marathon," although the course distance is nine-miles. The race boasts that the course remains "unchanged since 1908."

And that is part of the charm of this great race.

Thanksgiving Day may often feature a mixed bag of weather conditions in Pennsylvania. More often than not, the weather on race morning is challenging, to say the least. The 2010 edition of the race was contested during a driving sleet storm, reducing visibility, chilling runners to the bone with temperatures in the low thirties, transforming the Olympic-like event into one more akin to a downhill skiing competition.

After registration at the Moose Lodge, (no kidding), runners line up for the start, among a cheering throng of local citizens, many of whom have made an appearance at the race a part of their annual Thanksgiving celebration, as important to them as the turkey and cranberries. Some families have set up their lawn chairs, at the same location along the course, for generations.

For nearly the first two miles, the runners leave town and the adoring crowds, traversing the countryside over the gently rolling hills. As one nears the two-mile point in the race, the hill from hell looms. At two miles runners are racing at 600 feet above sea level. From two to three miles they ascend more than 300 feet, to 900 feet at the 1/3 mark of the race. Every inch of real estate between mile two and three is uphill. By three and a half, they have topped 1000 feet, and, after a short downhill, the apex of nearly 1100 feet is reached at the four and ¼ mile point. From there Berwick becomes a very fast course, with nearly five miles of net downhill to the finish, in town, a little shy of 600 feet above sea level. If one survives the first half of this race, good things usually follow.

What about the diamonds?

The top seven men receive diamond rings for their efforts; while the top seven women earn diamond necklaces. At the post race party, all runners warm up on hot soups and beverages as appetizers before they return home for their Thanksgiving feasts.

The Run for the Diamonds is one of those races you need to run at least once in your career. It is challenging, unique, and quaint. The race combines rural charm with a rugged course as well as an odd distance. Running it places you in the footsteps of Olympians as you become woven into the fabric of running history.

Buried deep within the coal country of northeast Pennsylvania lays the small borough of Shenandoah. 'King Coal,' the life blood of the town is long gone, and with it the many opportunities that created a 'boom town' in the early 20th century. Today, area employment is generally relegated to the Mrs. T's pierogy facility, and to the local farmer's fields, which have attracted many Mexican immigrants to the area.

If you've never consumed a pierogy, you are missing out on a delicious culinary treat. The tasty potato-filled pasta pocket is a delight to the taste buds. Boiled in butter, fried, smothered with onions, or doused with ketchup, pierogies both taste well and are nutritious. In addition, Tim Twardzik, one of the owners of the company, was a former hurdler, who attended the University of Notre Dame. His running roots have motivated him to become a sponsor at major marathons and Hawaii's Ironman Triathlon.

For the last thirty years, the Coal Cracker 10K race has grown to become an iconic running event.

During the Running Boom, a young group of local runners, led by two Shenandoah residents, Tom Talerico and Dan Lewis, started a running club, called the Shenandoah Flites. They also decided to conduct a race. A flat, fast course was out of the question, as the town of Shenandoah is carved from hilly, black mountains of coal. So, instead of trying to avoid the steep inclines that surround the town, they decided to embrace the challenges of the rugged terrain. The course they designed is among the most challenging 10Ks you will ever experience.

Beginning in the center of town, where many local residents gather on the hot, early June morning of the race, runners are euphoric as they proceed downhill for the first half mile or so of the race. Soon their enthusiasm is sapped by the steep hill that takes them out of town to the one mile mark of the race. From there, runners enjoy a fast, downhill mile to the two-mile marker. Next, the blacktop road ribbons through a series of rolling hills, snaking the participants through coal fields that produce a blast furnace effect, absorbing the June heat like a huge ebony sponge. Soon after the runners pass the four-mile mark, they make a left turn into hell. The Saint Nicholas Breaker hill is a long, steep climb, devoid of shade, surrounded with coal, which at that point in the race, may as well be hot lava rocks. A coal breaker is a large structure with a silo-like tower attached to it. At the top of the tower, coal would slide downhill along a conveyor belt, where impurities would be removed from the pure 'black gold,' and coal would be broken, (hence the name 'breaker') into various sizes. As the runners slog their way up the hill, for about one and a quarter miles, they observe the tarnished shell of the old breaker, which was constructed in 1930, and was, at one time, the largest coal breaker in the world, producing 12,500 tons of coal per day.

Near the top of the hill, competitors are not interested in the history of the anthracite coal industry, rather, they aim toward the rainbow ahead, produced by the spray from a huge fire hose, its contents arced high above in order to rain gently down on the runners.

A mile of the race remains after the hill is crested and a long, thigh-pounding downhill escorts runners back into town. After winding down the steep incline, the finish line comes into view. To the dismay of the already battered warriors, the finish line banner, adorned with the Mrs. T's logo, rests atop one final hill, a short but nasty incline that tests the runners' will until you cross the line.

Times are never fast. Tales are many, runners cross the line exhausted and frustrated, but the race consistently attracts nearly two-hundred runners annually.

It's not the difficulty of the course, rather the ambiance of this race that makes it successful. After the event, the post-race party at the local AMVETS Lodge is magnificent. Pierogies and beer are served until the last emaciated reveler is satisfied. Numerous awards, sculpted from coal, are presented at the awards ceremony.

Several years ago, a group of runners from Chambersburg made the two-hour trip north to participate in the Coal Cracker race. It wasn't their first time. They had run the race on several occasions because they enjoyed the challenging course and the hospitality afforded to them by the race organizers and the townspeople. After the post race party, the driver of the group experienced car trouble. Race Director Tim Talerico sent him to a local garage, the car was repaired, and the race directors covered the repair bill.

The Coal Cracker is a great race because of the great people who organize it.

I love the City of Philadelphia.

A two-hour drive south from 'upstate' where I reside, Philly is a cultural and sports center, our state's biggest city, home of the cheese steak, noted and feared for its ravenous and rowdy sports fans, and just a fun place to visit. It is also a great place to race at any time of the year.

Three of Philly's many road races standout as my personal favorites.

The Broad Street 10-Miler is held annually in May. A point-to-point course, takes competitors downhill, beginning at an elevation of one-hundred-seventy feet above sea level and finishing at an elevation of twelve feet. Runners are bussed to North Philadelphia, and run the entire length of Broad Street, finishing at the Philadelphia Naval Yard. Along the way they pass Temple University, run through some of the city's neighborhoods, around City Hall, where the statue of William Penn still keeps watch over his City of Brotherly Love, along the arts district to the finish near the sports complex, passing the docks where Rocky Balboa trained in the first Rocky film.

The first of the Philadelphia distance running trifecta, this is a must race if you enjoy a big-city race with a small-town feel.

In September, the ING Philadelphia Distance Run, now part of the Rock 'n' Roll Marathon series, will be run for the 34th consecutive year in 2011. One of the fastest, most scenic urban half marathons in the country, the race attracts more than 20,000 runners, partly due to its country setting in the middle of one of America's largest cities.

After a start on the Ben Franklin Parkway, with the Philadelphia Museum of Art looming in the background, runners snake past the birthplace of the nation, Independence Hall, before looping back to the parkway and onto to the largest inner-city park system in the U.S., Fairmount Park.

After completing a tour of downtown Philadelphia, for approximately four miles, runners cruise along the flat, shaded wide expanse of Kelly Drive, with the scenic Schuylkill River to their left, punctuated by views of the colorful boathouses, homes to the sculling teams that compete on the river, that dot the landscape along the way. A left turn onto the Fall's River Bridge is greeted by the twang of a local string band, famous for their gaudy attire and their strumming banjos featured in a strut down Broad Street on New Year's Day in the annual Mummer's Parade. From the nine-mile point, the race winds along peaceful Martin Luther King Boulevard. Here, one feels like one is running on a quiet country road, rather than racing in America's fifth largest city.

The statue of Rocky Balboa, Philadelphia's gritty, blue-collar hero, greets the participants at the finish line, in front of the Philadelphia Museum of Art, where some runners still have the stamina to recreate Rocky's celebratory triumphant sprint up to the top of the Art Museum steps.

Throughout this tour of Philadelphia, runners change elevation by no more than thirty feet, which explains why this is a record-setting course and ranks as a great race.

Completing the triple crown of races in the City of Brotherly Love is the Philadelphia Marathon, held annually on the Sunday before Thanksgiving.

Following much of the same course as the Philadelphia Distance Run, this race is ideally designed for both the novice as well as the seasoned runner. It is scenic, flat, and fast. The race feels urban; but much of it runs like a jaunt through the country. It is spectator-friendly, with several family checkpoints, a large viewing area at the half marathon mark, and a fast finish on the Ben Franklin Parkway, the Museum of Art to your back, with City Hall in your view.

Along the way runners pass Independence Hall, follow the Delaware River, skirt the perimeter of the Philadelphia Zoo, and turn around in the quaint suburb of Manayunk, before returning home on Kelly Drive.

Within a two-hour drive of my home, nestled in the coal-scarred hills of northeastern Pennsylvania, these great races cover every major distance from Five-Kilometers to the marathon. My great races probably aren't much different from your great races. Whether one lives in Alabama or Alaska; Maine or Minnesota, on virtually every weekend, one can find a great race in one's own back yard.

MILE 18–BOSTON

The young woman behind the desk in the cramped lobby of the Fenway Motel looked concerned, Before her stood a gaunt figure with sunken eyes, reeking of stale sweat, and caked with salt. A shiny space blanket, issued to him at the finish line, hung from his shoulders like a super hero's cape, crinkling with each movement. The unicorn medal, bearing an '82,' signifying the number of annual Boston Marathon races, hung from his neck, his badge of honor, earned by virtue of having completed his first Boston Marathon.

The long walk from the finish line at the Prudential Center to the Fens had been more like a painful shuffle, robbing him of his last few ounces of stamina. He needed the key to his room, where a bed and a warm shower awaited.

Suddenly, like a bolt of lightning, a plier-like vise grip bit into his weakened right hamstring. A cramp, the kind that strikes without warning in the middle of the night, seized him. A painful, silent grimace crossed his face.

At that moment, as if reaching out to the helpless soul who stood before her, the desk clerk asked, "May I help you?" White-hot pain consumed him. He gripped the marble desk top. Before he could summon enough strength to reply, a middle-aged man, who just couldn't grasp the mentality of those who run 26.2 miles for fun, joined the attendant behind the desk. He glanced at the pained figure before him, and in his Boston accent drawled, "Not unless yaw name is Gawd!"

Despite a debilitating leg cramp and a wise guy at the hotel desk, on that third Monday of April in 1978, my love affair with the Boston Marathon began.

Perhaps my fondness of history draws me to a place that declares a holiday celebrating the day that seventy farmers stood up to seven-hundred British Regulars on the Lexington Green, shed blood at the North Bridge in Concord, then chased the redcoats back to Boston, igniting a war that would separate America from Great Britain and launch us on the path to freedom.

Maybe it's the charm of Betty, the receptionist, at the hotel in Braintree, who, on the Saturday before the 2010 Boston Marathon, instructed me where to 'paak my caa.'

It could be the Irish punk sounds of Boston's Dropkick Murphys, the blue, green and orange lines of the MBTA, (Massachusetts Bay Transportation Authority), the sight of Fenway Park's Citgo sign beckoning as the race winds down, the screaming girls at Wellesley, or the army of boisterous spectators that swells in every town along the way, then increases and erupts as you enter the city. The crowd that, more than any other marathon crowd in any other city, displays a genuine respect for every runner, and treats each competitor like an Olympic champion.

Whether it's a single reason, or a combination of many, the Boston Marathon, in my opinion, is the greatest footrace on the planet.

Here's why.

Hopkinton, the starting line, became a town in 1715. Ashland, at the three-mile mark, was settled in 1750. Framingham, at mile six was settled in 1650, Natick in 1651, Wellesley, at the half way point, in 1660, and Newton, where the famed hills begin, in 1630. Each step of the Boston Marathon takes the runners through some of the oldest communities in the country.

Then there's the rich history of the race itself.

On Patriot's Day, April 19, 1897, fifteen runners covered the 24.5 mile distance from Metcalf's Mill in Ashland to the Irvington Oval in Boston. John J. McDermott was the first winner of the Boston Marathon. His time of two hours, 55 minutes, 10 seconds, was nearly seven minutes ahead of his closest competitor. In all, fifteen men competed in the first Boston race.

In 1908 the official Olympic distance of 26.2 miles, the distance from Windsor Castle to the Olympic Stadium in London, was set, and in 1924, the Boston Marathon conformed with the Olympic standard, moving the starting line to Hopkinton. Clarence DeMar earned his third consecutive Boston Marathon victory that year, smashing the world record by blistering the new course in a time of 2:29:40. DeMar went on to win a record seven Boston Marathons, and earned a bronze medal in the marathon at the 1924 Paris Olympic Games. DeMar deservedly earned the moniker, 'Mr. DeMarathon.'

DeMar may hold the Boston Marathon record with seven victories, but it is the man from West Medford, Massachusetts, who finished second a record seven times, earned the adulation of runners around the world, and was named by Runner's World magazine as the Runner of the Century, who became synonymous with the venerable race.

Johnny Kelley notched his first of two Boston Marathon victories in 1935, after having endured a second place finish the year before. Kelley became the favorite to win the 1936 race. He did not, but the story of his defeat is richly steeped in Boston Marathon folklore.

Climbing the last of the Newton Hills, Kelley, who had lagged behind the leader, Elison 'Tarzan' Brown, a Narragansett Indian, whose shoes fell apart at the twenty-one mile mark of the previous year's race, surged up the incline, apparently catching the frontrunner. At that point, Kelley, by all accounts a sportsman, tapped Brown on the back as a sign of respect. Brown, however, construed the gesture as a taunt, and became infuriated. The Indian then sprinted down the other side of the hill, into the city, breaking both Kelley's will and his heart.

The site of running's most famous pat on the back is forever known as Heartbreak Hill.

Kelley went on to win the 1945 Boston Marathon, and he placed in the top five a remarkable fifteen times between 1934 and 1950. He also ran in two Olympic Games, at Berlin in 1936, where he finished 18th, and in London, at age forty, in 1948, where he placed 21st.

In 1992, at the age of eighty-four, he ran his last full Boston Marathon. That race represented his 61st start at Boston, with fifty-eight finishes. He ran the last seven miles of the race for the next two years.

In 1993, a statue of the distance running icon was erected, on the Boston Marathon course, in Newton, about a mile before the base of Heartbreak Hill. Kelley, who died in 2004, at the age of ninety-seven, still presides over the race participants as they pass through the town of Newton.

Runners from Southeast Asia dominated the Boston Marathon from the late 1940s to the mid-1950s. Then, in 1953, Keizo Yamada, from Japan, shattered the world record, taking it into the teens, clocking a 2:18:51.

Finns took over the mantle of victory at Boston, winning the race in 1954, 1956, 1959, 1960, 1961, and 1962.

Roberta Gibb is recognized as the first female Boston Marathon finisher. In 1966, she sent in her race entry blank, but was refused because she was a woman. She ran, unofficially, and finished the race in a time of 3:21:40. She ran unofficially again in 1967, finishing an hour ahead of Katherine Switzer. Switzer attempted to enter the race officially, under the neutral title of 'K.V. Switzer. Race official, Jock Semple, incensed by what he viewed as blatant deception, sprung out of the crowd and attempted to physically remove her from the race, shouting, "Get the hell out of my race and give me those numbers." Switzer's boyfriend shoved Semple, sending him careening back into the crowd from which he had emerged. The photograph of the sexist incident made national headlines.

Women were finally officially allowed to run the Boston Marathon in 1972. Nina Kuscsik bested seven other women to win that race in a time of 3:10:26.

In 1970, the Boston Marathon took a bold step by introducing qualifying standards to the event. One was now required to submit a legitimate qualifying time in order to enter the race. Being the first race of its kind to actually turn people away, the move piqued interest in the Boston Marathon. Suddenly, everyone was attempting to 'qualify.'

While Frank Shorter's Olympic marathon victory in 1972 may have ignited the Running Boom, it was Bill Rodgers' Boston Marathon triumph in 1975 that fueled the fire.

The easy-going, blonde-haired Rodgers had turned in a modest time of 2:19:34, placing 14th the previous year, but training up to one-hundred-thirty miles a week, often on the Newton Hills had prepared him for a breakthrough race.

In 1975, Rodgers stunned the world at the Boston Marathon, obliterating the course record, with a time of 2:09:55. What's most remarkable about his time is that he completely stopped four times at water stations and once to tie his shoe.

The Boston field topped two-thousand competitors that year. West German Liane Winter set the women's world record, with a time of 2:42:24, and the Wheelchair Division of the race began, with Bob Hall covering the course in 2:58:00

Bill Rodgers went on to win the Boston Marathon in 1978, 1979, and 1980. In 1979 he lowered his course record to a 2:09:27. Today, at age sixty-three, he is a prostate cancer survivor. He still trains and competes regularly. Rodgers, who also won four New York City Marathons, continues to serve as an ambassador for the sport of long distance running. He has never lost his humility, and remains one of the true 'good guys' in the entire sports world.

Bill Rodgers, one of the greatest marathoners of all times, sums up his life best with a quote that from which we can all benefit. "To be a consistent winner means not just preparing for just one day, one month or even a year–but for a lifetime."

The third Monday in April can bring an array of weather conditions to the eastern United States. More often than not, the temperatures in Boston on that day are cool, raw, and damp, but in 1976, record heat descended upon the east coast. For most folks the summer like heat was delightful, but for the one-thousand-eight-hundred-ninety-eight runners at the Boston Marathon on that day, the ninety-eight-degree thermometer reading at the starting line led to a forty- percent attrition rate. Jack Fultz was one of the survivors, crossing the finish line in a sunbaked time of 2:20:19.

By 1979 the Running Boom was in full swing, attracting a record crowd of seven-thousand-eight hundred-seventy-nine runners to Boston. More than three-thousand runners broke the three-hour barrier in that race. That's right, over three-thousand! Better still, fifty-one broke 2:20, in what, statistically, may have been the marathon with the greatest depth of times in the history of the sport.

A young Joan Benoit, a student at Bowdoin College, set an American women's marathon record, with a 2:35:15 performance at the 1979 event.

Baseball had its steroid scandal; long distance running had Rosie Ruiz.

It is painful for me to write about this. First, the 1980 Boston Marathon was the only marathon in my career, and the one of fourteen Boston Marathons I have participated in, that I failed to complete. A nagging back injury caused me to drop at the sixteen-mile mark of the race. From there I hobbled to the Massachusetts Turnpike, where I hitched a ride back into the city.

Well, as it turned out, the apparent race winner, a somewhat out of shape, toneless, amazingly fresh looking woman by the name of Rosie Ruiz, never completed the race either.

In an age prior to chip-timing or camera monitoring, this fraud apparently emerged from the crowd on Commonwealth Avenue, about a half mile from the finish line. She reveled in the adulation of the thousands of spectators, most of whom, naturally, believed she had conquered the challenging course, and was now on her way to victory. Ruiz completed the deception with waves to the crowd, and even accepted the ceremonial laurel wreath presented to the race winners.

She was disqualified from the race later in the week, when a body of evidence indicated that she had deceived just about everyone, robbing the spotlight from the true victor.

The real winner of the race, a petite gracious Canadian, Jacqueline Gareau, was eventually, declared the winner. Her time of 2:34:28 was a new course record. Race officials ceremoniously allowed her to cross the finish line a week later.

Thanks to the despicable actions of Rosie Ruiz, intensive video surveillance and computer monitoring were instituted at Boston and all major road races.

The 1982 Boston Marathon will forever be remembered as "The Duel in the Sun."

Traditionalists at the Boston Athletic Association stubbornly refused to budge on the Noon starting time of the race, and the conditions at the starting line were arid. The sky was cloudless, and the sun became red-hot orb by early morning, punishing runners not yet acclimatized to the heat after a brutal northeastern winter.

I was pleased with my time of 2:28:43 at the race, but my most significant pain in the twenty-four or so hours after my finish resulted from the bright pink lines of sunburn which outlined the perimeter of my race singlet as well as on my ankles above the sock line.

For sixteen miles it was a three-man race. Four time race winner Bill Rodgers battled with the young, brash, two-time New York City Marathon champion, Alberto Salazar, and a soft-spoken Midwesterner, Minnesota's Dick Beardsley.

The pace was as hot as the day itself, as the dry temperatures climbed into the high 70s.

The first victim among the leaders was Rodgers, who fell off the pace at sixteen miles. It was now a two-man race. Salazar, clearly the favorite, attempted to break his rival on the Newton Hills, but Beardsey hung tough, unfazed. The crowds were frenetic as the duel continued down the long stretch of Commonwealth Avenue. Beardsley had a slight edge when, near the Eliot Lounge, with less than a mile to go to the finish, his hamstring locked. Salazar, the best marathoner in the world at that time, seized the moment and captured the lead. But the race was far from over. Within a hundred yards of the onset of his hamstring cramp, Beardsley encountered a major source of irritation to most drivers: a pothole. Like most drivers, he hit it . . . with his bad leg. Miraculously, the jolt somehow loosened the hamstring and the battle was, again, on. Beardsley drew even with Salazar. The final stretch of race real estate on Boylston Street became crazed by the deafening cheers of the crowd, as the two champions sprinted to the finish line, flanked by motorcycle police, with Salazar emerging the victor. Both men had smashed the course record. Salazar clocked a time of 2:08:52 and Beardsley followed a mere two seconds back at 2:08:54. It was the first time two men had broken 2:09 in the same race.

Salazar, however, paid a steep price for his victory. Severely dehydrated, his body temperature dropped to a near fatal eighty-eight degrees, and it took several liters Intravenous fluids to stabilize him. By Salazar's own admission he was never the same after that race.

In 1983, the Boston Marathon reached its peak in attracting an incredible depth of running talent. Marathons were springing up everywhere, and most were offering prize money. Boston held steady in remaining an 'amateur' race, but the times were changing.

For me, the 1983 race was unforgettable. I achieved my personal best marathon time of 2:22:54, a mark that would win many marathons today. At Boston, in 1983, however, it earned me 125th place.

As I made the turn onto Boyleston Street, icy chills shot down my spine as I realized I would achieve my personal best, and possibly break the 2:23 barrier. What's more, the crowd was as excited as I. I've always loved the enthusiasm of the Boston Marathon spectators, but could it be that they were cheering wildly for me, recognizing I was about to complete my personal best marathon performance?

Nah!

It seems that someone had stolen my thunder.

For the entire race, a female had been ahead of me. It was inconceivable to me that, at that time, a woman could turn in a time of less than two hours 23 minutes, but I was wrong.

Joan Benoit, who ran the first half of the race at a 2:17 pace, shattered the world record by more than two minutes, running a time of 2:22:43. It was she, not I, for whom the crowd cheered.

Greg Meyer captured the men's race. He is the last American to win the Boston Marathon.

The 1985 race marked the end of the 'old' Boston Marathon. Still devoid of prize money, top marathoners went elsewhere, and the race was won by England's Geoff Smith in a time of 2:14:05. It would mark the last time the race would finish at the Prudential Center, as John Hancock Financial Services would take over as the chief race sponsor. The next year prize money was offered, and Australia's Rob deCastella cashed in big-time. He crushed the course record with a time of 2:07:51. Norway's Ingrid Kristiansen took home the women's prize with a time of 2:24:55.

In 1988 the African Revolution began at Boston. That year marked the closest finish in race history, as Kenya's Ibrahim Hussein and Tanzania's Juma Ikangaa battled for 26 miles, and 285 yards, with Hussein outsprinting his rival in the final one-hundred-meters, to win in a time of 2:08:43, a one second margin of victory.

By 1990, the field of competitors at the Boston Marathon had swelled to 9,362. Italy's Gelindo Bordin broke Boston's Olympic jinx by becoming the first men's Olympic marathon winner to also capture a victory at Boston. His time was 2:08:09.

1994 was a record-setting year at Boston. Kenya's Cosmos Ndeti broke Rob deCastella's course record, by turning in a time of 2:07:15. Germany's Uta Pippig shattered Olympic champion Joan Benoit-Samuelson's course record by nearly a minute, with a time of 2:21:54

The Centennial edition of the Boston Marathon was held on April 15, 1996. Several days before the race a spring snowstorm had dumped more than a foot of snow on the Boston area. Race officials, in preparation for the largest field ever to run the race, used helicopters to dry off the staging area in and around the starting line at Hopkinton.

Officially, 38,708 competitors entered the race legally. Estimates, including unofficial runners, ran as high as over 40,000. Remarkably, 35,868 runners finished the race. The first to cross the finish line were Moses Tanui and Uta Pippig, but the real winners were the near 36,000 runners who earned the indelible stamp of crossing the finish line on the historic anniversary of an historic race.

At the first Boston Marathon of the new century, three runners made the final turn onto Boyleston Street together. The finish turned out to be the closest in Boston Marathon history. Elijah Lagat outsprinted former Boston Marathon champion and fellow Kenyan countryman, Moses Tanui, as well as Ethiopian Gezahenge Abera. Lagat and Abera were awarded the exact same times of 2:09:47, in what amounted to a photo finish; while Tanui posted a 2:09:50.

The women's race mirrored the men, with Catherine Ndereba crossing the finish line in 2:26:11, followed by Irina Bogacheva, and Fatuma Roba, who both registered times of 2:26:27, the closest women's finish in race history.

Kenyan Margaret Okayo smashed the women's course record in 2002, with an incredible time of 2:20:53, with Robert Kiprono Cheruiyot lowering the men's record in 2010, running a 2:05:52.

At this writing, however, the Boston Marathon record has reached a new level of excellence.

Under perfect weather conditions at the 2011 Boston Marathon, Kenya's Geoffrey Mutai astounded the world marathon community by running the fastest marathon time in history. His 2:03:02 stands as a remarkable running accomplishment, representing a pace of around 4:45 per mile.

Ryan Hall obliterated the American record in the same race. His time of 2:04:58 earned him 4th place.

Since 1988, Kenyan runners have captured nineteen Boston Marathon titles. These incredible athletes train hard, lead remarkably Spartan lives, eat little red meat, train at high altitude, and have a burning desire to succeed at earning a living while doing something they love, when most of their countrymen earn an average of about $7,000 a year.

Long before we coined the term 'globalization,' the Boston Marathon was global. The winner of the second Boston Marathon in 1898 was a Canadian, and, in its one-hundred-fifteen-year history winners have hailed from every inhabited continent. Baseball may have its World Series, but Boston is, indeed, the World's Marathon.

My fourteen Boston Marathons have ranked among some of the favorite and best races of my life as a runner. Except for the 1980 failure, I have never had a bad race at Boston.

The hospitality of the New Englanders who love their marathon like they love their Red Sox, has been incredible.

A corporate executive once opened up his home to a group of us in 1979. He threw in tickets for a Sox game. I sat along the first base line, seemingly able to reach out and touch the first base bag.

I've run along the rocky Maine coast, on Old Orchard Beach, during a stay on Marathon weekend.

Randy Haas and I, thanks to our sponsor, the now defunct Eastern Airlines, once spent race weekend at the posh Coplay Plaza Hotel near the finish line of the race

The Munier family of Newburyport graciously provided lodging for me on several occasions. In addition to getting me to and from the race on time, the patriarch of the family, Bob, served up post race homemade waffles, cooked on a century old, square waffle iron, the day after the race.

From waiters and waitresses, from race volunteers to Boston's Finest, folks in Beantown have always made this race special for me and the thousands of runners and their families who descend upon the city on race weekend.

In 1987, Haas and I had both turned in decent race performances. After the race we went to the Boston Beer Works, a tavern near Fenway Park. There we were greeted as conquering heroes. To Bostonians, finishing the Boston Marathon is the equivalent of reaching the Major Leagues. Running a time of sub 2:30 is like playing in the World Series.

Heck, runners ride the subway free on race day.

It's a Monday, but it's Patriot's Day, so only in the states of Maine and Massachusetts do people have the day off from work and school. Many of them are stationed somewhere along the race course.

If you're a runner, then, the Boston Marathon is sensational, in that it stimulates one's senses.

At Hopkinton a sign reads, 'It All Begins Here.'

As you emerge from the busses that transport the runners to the starting line, the air is pungent with the odor of muscle gels and job johnnies. The loudspeaker blares with music and incessant announcements.

At the starting line runners are tightly cramped, and no matter what the temperature, body odor is rampant. That rivulet of water that just enveloped your feet is probably urine from runners behind you who need to relieve themselves one final time. Depending where you are in the crowd, you may or may not hear the starting gun, rather, you follow the crowd and slowly shuffle until you reach the blue and yellow emblem at the starting line.

Your adrenalin courses through your body as you weave through the congestion of the first couple of miles. The greatest elevation drop on the entire course occurs in the first mile, where you plummet one-hundred-thirty feet. You stride effortlessly on the downhill, and then you nearly stop as you encounter runner roadblocks in front of you. Local folks line the narrow road, some extending their hands in anticipation of a slap from a runner. Fraternity houses blast music while their inhabitants toast your efforts. Springsteen's 'Born to Run,' and the 'Chariots of Fire' theme songs are still popular tunes. Crowds swell near the Ashland clock tower around the four-mile mark and again at the Framingham Train Depot at mile six. From there you settle in as the hills roll, until you enter the town of Natick at mile ten.

Crowds become sporadic in a prelude to one of the most electric portions of the race.

It starts as a high-pitched buzz, followed by a town sign, then bedlam that quickens the pace of all runners. At the exact half way point in the race, the girls from Wellesley College line both sides of the race course. If you've ever watched the grainy, black and white videos of the early Beatles' concerts, you have an idea of the shrill, frenzied cheers that emanate from the enthusiastic coeds. Male runners go crazy. Many a Wellesley girl has received a sweat soaked kiss from a middle-aged male runner. The volume and pitch seem to rise when a female runner passes. Wellesley serves as a farewell to the predominately downhill, relatively easy course completed, and the monster challenge yet to come.

The Newton Hills begin around mile sixteen. If you hail from my part of the world these inclines are far from intimidating, but their placement in the race is. Thighs that have suffered damage from many downhill portions of the course fatigue easily on the Newton Hills. After the first three hills, the fourth, and final, infamous Heartbreak Hill, does, indeed become a challenge. It rises eighty eight feet over a half mile stretch, and it appears between miles twenty and twenty one. Sadistic crowds, twenty to thirty spectators deep, line both sides of Heartbreak Hill, screaming words of encouragement to fatigued runners.

Once you've conquered the Newton Hills, though, the best is yet to come.

A long downhill takes runners past Boston College onto a flat stretch of road, where the city crowds continue to grow. In the distance, Fenway Park's Citgo sign looms, as does the crowd, infused by the Red Sox fans exiting the ball game that began at 11:00 a.m. Two Kilometers along the long stretch of Commonwealth Avenue, and the finish line nears. Spectators cheer your name, as they have all along the route. Many Boston Marathon spectators have newspaper in hand, eager to match a number with your name.

Abruptly, you make a right on Hereford Street. It is almost deserted, little more than an alley.

Near the finish of the world's most famous marathon, there is a momentary letdown as nearly twenty-five and a half miles of screaming spectators have dwindled to a handful. Hereford Street is the tunnel that leads you into the stadium.

A left onto Boylston Street and all the training miles become worth it. The dank winter days when the icy wind sliced your face and the darkness seemed to envelope you out of nowhere. The twenty-mile runs, where you dragged yourself out of bed in the freezing temperatures, and you hobbled around for the rest of the day as if you were preparing for your 100th birthday party.

The two jello-pops you call your legs spring back to life as you feel as though you've come out of the tunnel at the Rose Bowl or you've just hit the home run to win the World Series. You are punched by the roar of the more than 50,000 people who line the wide thoroughfare, their thundering cheers punctuated by the clanging sound of cowbells and, to them, you are the Olympic champion. Goose bumps emerge all over your sweat drenched body. Blow kisses to the adoring crowds, give them a bicep flex, or cup your hand to your ear, like I have, and the cheers become deafening. You hit the 26-mile mark and you look for your family. In the crowd, through your tears of joy, you can usually pick them out. You cross the finish line spent. Often elated, sometimes disappointed. The medal is placed around your neck.

You have followed a trail of 115 years of Boston Marathon champions.

Now, YOU are a Boston Marathon champion.

MILE 19–AGING

"Growing old is something you do if you're lucky."
Groucho Marx

Six years ago, at age fifty-one, I participated in a small, local race, that drew around one hundred competitors. The 5K event featured rolling hills, with a fast, three-hundred-meter downhill finish. Approximately half way through the race it became apparent that I had the opportunity to win, if I could hold off two local high school runners. The lure of an attractive silver bowl to place on my mantle served to quicken my pace. A little more than a half mile from the finish, we climbed a long hill. My legs ached from fatigue, my lungs burned like the lit-end of a cheap cigar, but my old and experienced brain worked overtime, devising the winning strategy. Early in my fifth decade of life, it was unlikely that I could match the swift, fast-twitch muscles of an eighteen-year-old, so to think I had the ability to out sprint the youngsters was pure folly. Instead, I summoned up enough energy to plow up the hill, knees raised high, arms pumping, chest heaving. By the time I reached the crest of the hill, I had put thirty meters between myself and the two young men, negating their ability to turn the race into a one hundred-meter dash. Steadily, I glided to the finish line, breaking the tape in victory.

Just as aging baseball pitchers can no longer rely solely on their fastball to get them through the game, aging runners must also make adjustments in their racing strategy in order to continue to successfully compete against their younger rivals.

The most difficult challenge for an aging competitive runner is the acceptance of declining performance. There is no exact age at which race times slow, although most runners reach their peak in their thirties. As a runner ages, race times are going to progressively get slower. The key to success as one ages, then, is to minimize the slide. In order to do so, adjustments must be made in training methods. Theories and advice may abound, but the simple fact is, find the training regimen that works for you, at whatever stage you are in your chronological life, and follow it.

In my early thirties I would routinely turn in ninety to one- mile-training weeks, along with a hard speed workout on the track. Twenty-mile training runs in preparation for a marathon were logged at around a six-minute per mile pace. My race times generally reflected my hard work. Foolishly, however, I attempted to continue this aggressive training method into my 40s, and was rewarded with numerous injuries and much frustration.

As we age, our healing process slows down. The old post-marathon axiom of, "one day to recover for each mile of the race," doubles if you're in your fiftiess. Rest becomes very important to the aging runner. If you've been an everyday runner, perhaps six days a week, with a rest day thrown in is a good idea. Also, make sure your easy days are REAL easy. On my easy days I might run with my dogs, or zig zag on secluded mountain trails, with little regard for clocking a fast time.

Accept the inevitable and adjust. Set reasonable, challenging, yet attainable race goals for yourself. There's not a geezer out there who isn't thrilled each time we pass a twenty-something runner in a race, but as one races into their fifties and beyond, it's more important to capture the age division honors. Measure yourself against runners in your particular age bracket.

It's a great sport. When you're fifty-four, that fifty-fifth birthday isn't quite as painful when you know you're going to be the youngster in the next age division.

Age may require you to adjust your racing plans as well. I still enjoy training for, and racing marathons. Personally, I have jettisoned the 5K distance. I'd rather race longer distances. Most runners, however, have tapered their racing in the other direction. If you're running mostly 5K's as you age, cut down on your mileage and spend more time on the track. Work on quality rather than quantity and the results will be amazing. Check out local race results. Many 5K races these days are being won by runners in their forties and fifties..

Indeed, competitive running is entering a completely uncharted area. Runners have never competed at such a high level for so long.

At age fifty-four, 1984 Olympic marathon champion, and former world record holder, Joan Benoit Samuelson, at this writing, is less than a minute away from smashing the two hour, 50 minute barrier, which will qualify her for the U.S. Olympic Trials in the marathon, nearly thirty years after having becoming the first Olympic women's marathon winner in history.

Philadelphia's Bob Schwelm has flirted with the 2:30 marathon mark at age fifty-one, but has been unable to match the astounding performance of Norm Green, who clocked a time of 2:25:51, at age fifty-two. Green, from Valley Forge, Pennsylvania, went on to run a 2:27:42 at age fifty-five in 1987, making him the oldest American to ever break 2:30 at the marathon distance.

In 2008, sixty-year year-old Japanese marathoner, Yoshihisha Hosaka, became the fastest person of his age ever to run a marathon, when he blazed a 2:31:19, crushing the age-group world record by one minute, 45 seconds, at the Beppu Oita Mainichi Marathon.

Our life spans are increasing, our training methods are more sophisticated, and sports medicine capabilities are astounding. All evidence indicates that age group records will continue to plummet.

But becoming an aging runner doesn't require you to enter races. Few activities keep the mind and body as healthy as the years pile on as a regular running regimen.

Maintaining that regular running routine, however, may not be so easy, so as you age, you must grasp for every bit of assistance available to you, as it is often necessary to cheat Father Time.

Over the past couple of years, I had come to detest the beginning of my training runs. My legs were stiff and my breathing left me gasping for air as if someone had stuffed cotton in my lungs. To solve the problem, I now slowly jog ½ to 3/4 mile BEFORE I meet my training partners. By the time we hit our watches, I have coursed some blood through my body, loosened my legs and expanded my lungs.

Stretching becomes more important as we age. That being said, I hate to stretch, I'm woeful, and years of long distance running has left me about as supple as an icicle. Still, upon the insistence of my wife, who intensely stretches before her workouts, I have attempted to stretch both before and after my training runs, and my injuries have diminished.

Every aging runner has his or her 'Achilles heel.' I actually suffered from achilles tendinitis to the point where I walked down the steps sideways each morning. Metaphorically speaking, however, the

'Achilles heel' often manifests itself in the form of lower back pain, knee problems, iliotibial band syndrome, quadriceps strains, or the demon of all age-related running ailments, hamstring issues.

Simple weighted leg lifts will strengthen quads and remove stress from overworked hamstrings

Don't be afraid to take advantage of all that's available to you. Make sure you have a good medical doctor who knows something about running. Be sure to have good chiropractor and podiatrist.

For a small investment of around $100 I bought a portable ultrasound wand as well as an electrical stimulation machine. Purchased around a year ago, they have paid many dividends in a short amount of time.

Take whatever supplements you and your physicians decide work for you. I take fish oil tablets daily for my joint and heart health, and have recently begun to take COQ 10, having studied some of the research on its oxygen-replenishing effects.

Keep ibuprofen on hand, drink plenty of fluids all the time, and have some type of analgesic balm available for those daily aches and pains.

Hit the trails when you can to save your legs, and on some workouts, just go out and enjoy. Running can be more relaxed and less intense as we age.

Continuing to run in the Golden Years is an excellent insurance policy, but it does not make us invincible. Plaque in our arteries, the ever-looming threat of cancer that can attack any of us at any time caution us to remain vigilant and to take all other precautions, screenings, and examinations in order to maintain good health.

Throughout my adult life, running has not become like a job to me. It is something I look forward to. It is something that I need. Sure there are days when I dread the upcoming workout, but I dread it more if I don't do it.

There's nothing quite like exploring that secluded part of the beach, where the only imprints in the sand are those left by your running shoes, the frozen fear that causes your spine to melt when a pheasant waits to the very moment you're upon it before it takes flight, or taking your first steps out the door in the dark and returning to a brilliant sunrise and the promise of a new day.

On an unusually warm December day, just past the Winter Solstice, daylight slipped away as I crested a hill in Saint Clair, a small town at the base of a mountain, five miles north of my home. The air was still, a semicircle of sun strained over the horizon, as I loped down the incline. Suddenly, from the heavens it seemed, church bells chimed, "Angels We Have Heard on High." It was actually the bells from the church down the road, but it reminded me of the personal spirituality each day's run produces.

In a big city or at a vacation resort, an early morning run beats a GPS street locator any day. Last year, at the Isle of Palms, South Carolina, a sunrise run took me past a lazy beach bar from which emanated the tantalizing smell of bacon. I returned to the condo to announce to my wife that I had located our breakfast destination. What resulted was a magnificent Cajun-style breakfast as we watched the shrimp boats trawling off the South Carolina coast.

There's no better way to tour a big city than by running through it. I've run through the tunnel inside Philadelphia's City Hall, past the Liberty Bell and Independence Hall, solemnly in front of Washington's Vietnam Memorial, and through the Boston Common.

My ninety-year old mother thinks I should have quit running twenty years ago. She frequently reminds me with greater emphasis by warning, "Running's going to put you in your grave."

Although I'm counting on that not happening for another forty years or so, it's probably not a bad way to go.

MILE 20–THE BEST

Anchored to the back of the old pickup truck was a large megaphone. As we ran, festive Christmas carols blared from the device. The early December air was crisp and clear. Puffs of steam rose from our mouths as we exhaled. The hill was steep, but Randy Haas and I talked and joked, all alone, leading a field of two-hundred runners at the 1986 Reading, Pennsylvania's annual Jingle Bell 10K.

I knew my days were numbered. I realized my time was about to expire. With two miles to go in the race, my friend and training partner had been polite. He had run conservatively in the early stages of the race, fully cognizant that his short apprenticeship had come to an end. Now, however, it was time to take the first step back in his return to his former greatness. As we glided down the hill, he accelerated slowly. Nothing was said. 'Deck the Halls' and rhythmic breathing were the only sounds. My strides, as long, but not nearly as efficient as his, were woefully inadequate. By the five-mile point the race was over. At the finish line his lead over me exceeded a minute. My time was thirty-one minutes, 43 seconds. His was 30:30. I felt no animosity, no regret. I had run my best. I was just defeated by the best.

During the late 1970s and early 1980s, Blue Mountain High School, nestled in the hills of central Pennsylvania, just south of the anthracite coal field, was a running powerhouse. In a region dominated by high school football, the Pennsylvania Dutch work ethic so prevalent in the area, extended into the sport of long distance running.

The Blue Mountain cross country team was led by their legendary coach, Ralph Jaeger. Jaeger, of German ancestry, sometimes known as, 'Herr Jaeger,' looked like a long distance runner, but was not. He was slightly built, thin and wispy. His ebony hair covered his forehead and rested above his glasses, which practically met his eyes. He was a chain-smoker, puffing on his cigarettes as he followed his runners on their routes.

Jaeger built his cross country teams into a local juggernaut, virtually unbeatable in local competition and always a contender at the State Championships.

Cross country became so popular at Blue Mountain that the team sometimes ran out of uniforms. Like Red Sox fans, who must wait for a death before obtaining a season ticket, Blue Mountain cross country runners had to hope the rigorous training would cause attrition, thus making a uniform available.

Attrition was a real possibility, as the requirement of the first practice in August was a hilly, eighteen-mile run from Blue Mountain High School, north to Pottsville and back. All cross country participants were required to complete the workout. Most were able to run the entire way, but for others, the trek took three hours or more.

As a freshman in high school, Randy Haas decided to play football. Standing close to six feet tall and weighing around 120 pounds, he was more suited to be a goal post rather than a squad member. He possessed speed, but few other attributes necessary to survive a game tailored for larger athletes.

In the spring he made the decision to run track, and soon it became apparent that he was a runner of extraordinary talent.

His thin, but emaciated chest, looking like a coat hanger covered with flesh, is a framework for an incredibly strong and efficient running machine. His resting pulse is so slow it might render him legally dead, and his large and efficient heart could power three men. In most of his race photographs his feet do not touch the ground. Rather, they glide, as if attached to a smooth belt that adjusts to speeds necessary for a particular race distance. His eyes are shark-like, dark and focused, as if constantly looking for prey that lurks at the finish line. He rarely looks side to side when he competes. His is a relentless quest to the end the race in the fastest possible manner. Throughout the race his breathing is imperceptible, and though he is covered in sweat at the finish line, he rarely looks tired. During daily workouts he talks incessantly, and he possesses the uncanny ability to lock into virtually any desired pace. For example, if we want to do a set of 400-meter repeats at a seventy-five-second pace, he will nail each one, within hundredths of a second. Mile intervals at a 5:15 pace? He'll hit them all within a second of the target time.

During his high school days, his incredible running attributes were honed on the track by a coach who was equally as skilled as cross country coach Jaeger.

Mark Herb, an 800 and a 1600-meter runner, who competed at Millersville University in southern Pennsylvania, put his distance runners through hellish workouts, informing them that they'd, "run 'til they puked." Often, they did, but these were the types of workouts on which Randy Haas thrived. Repeat sets of 12 x 400-meters, 8 x 800-meters, and ladder workouts were common, but cutting down the times on each interval made the workouts even more brutal.

Randy Haas excelled throughout his first three years as a high school runner. During his sophomore track season, in 1977, he was a member of the four x 800-meter relay team that placed second in the state, but in his senior year, he kicked his career into high gear. In the fall of 1979, he went undefeated with the exception of one-hundred meters of his entire season.

At the All League cross country meet, Haas held an insurmountable lead as he crested the final mound on the local golf course that served as the venue for the meet. Waves of intense heat radiated from the well-manicured fairway as he cruised toward the crowd gathered near the club house when, suddenly, his legs buckled and he collapsed to the turf, a victim of a heat stroke. He never finished the league meet, but went on to dominate the district meet, and in November, claimed the Pennsylvania state cross country championship, covering the 5-Kilometer course in fifteen-minutes, 54 seconds.

Throughout the spring of his senior year, Haas mowed down opponents in a methodical, efficient manner. At the state Track and Field Championships in May of 1980, he captured the 1600-Meter state championship with a time of 4:15.62, as well as the 800-Meter crown in a time of 1:54.35. His high school running career ended with three distance running state championships, a rare feat that has seldom been duplicated. Locally, his record times have stood for more than thirty years.

To the dismay of his coaches, the story of Randy Haas' promising running career ended, by his choosing, at the state championship meet.

Randy is a blue collar worker from a blue collar family. His father, Gerry, a scratch golfer, who, at age eighty, still shoots his age, worked in a local aluminum manufacturing plant. So, despite the efforts of his coaches to dissuade him, Haas chose to decline college for the working world, opting to accept employment at a nearby factory.

The story of Randy Haas' running career almost ended there, but it was really only beginning.

After nearly a six-year hiatus from running, a time period in which, for most folks, the waistline would grow and competitive ambition would shrink, Haas decided to become a runner again.

In early 1986 we began to train together.

At his first race in the summer of that year, I prevailed, but I realized my edge over him would be temporary. By December's Jingle Bell 10K he had passed me for the last time and he would never look back.

Randy Haas, the three-time Pennsylvania state champion was back. This time, however, he returned as the 'blue collar' champion.

He settled into his job at a local plastic manufacturing facility, where he worked eight-hour shifts, a position he's held for the past twenty-four years. What's more, he works the 'swing shift,' meaning he constantly rotates from the 8-4, 4-12, and the 12-8, midnight, or "graveyard" shift. He stands as a legend at his job, but not for his running accomplishments. Haas accepts virtually every hour of overtime offered to him. More remarkably, his overtime hours are offered in four-hour blocks, which transform his eight-hour shifts into twelve-hour marathons.

For most folks, this disruption of sleep patterns would render consistent training impossible, but Haas has thrived on it. At the Reading Hospital 10K, forty-five minutes south of his workplace, he once completed his midnight shift at 8:00 a.m., showed up at the starting line five minutes before the race, and bested the field of eight-hundred runners in a time of less than 31 minutes.

During the next several years, Haas ripped through local races like Sherman's troops tore through the South, decimating any competitor in his path.

His 5K times consistently fell less than 15 minutes, and on a trip to Florida in 1992, he took advantage of the flat, fast circuit at the Festival of Lights 5K in Fort Myers and clocked his personal best 5K time of 14:02 in front of a crowd of more than 25,000 spectators who were lined up to watch the Festival of Lights parade.

The former 800-meter champion displayed amazing range. He blasted a time of 23:52 at the five-mile distance, and a 29:36 for the 10K.

At the 1991 Philadelphia Distance Run, his time of 1:06:52 at the half marathon distance earned him second place among Americans.

Although the marathon was never his favorite distance, he distinguished himself with a 2:17:36, his personal best, at the 1992 Boston Marathon

In 1995 he traveled to Grandma's Marathon in Duluth, Minnesota. There he qualified for the Olympic Trials marathon, by clocking a time of 2:21:46. He participated in the Trials in January 1996, in Charlotte, North Carolina.

Randy Haas and I have trained together for the past twenty-five years. He is, by far, the most gifted runner I have ever encountered. He is also a basic, no-frills runner. His blue collar work ethic applies to his daily training. During our peak training period in the 1980s and 1990s, we would routinely log ninety-mile weeks, pounding out long runs of eighteen to twenty miles, which were always done at a brisk, near marathon race pace. Speed workouts on the track were conducted in the middle of the week, and featured intense repetitions of 400 or 800 meters for short races, and mile repeats for the longer ones.

The rest of our week would include a tempo-type run, and once or twice a week we would run easy, talking and joking while turning in workouts of eight to twelve miles.

We took our racing very seriously. When we'd race, it always meant something to us. If we did well, we knew our training methods were working. If not, we worked on adjustments to our regimen. There were no excuses. Haas, always known to vocalize his opinions, neither offered, nor accepted explanations for a poor performance. He had no problem instructing an excuse-filled runner whom he had just defeated that perhaps he should simply, "train harder," or, "race less."

Randy and his wife Lisa have earned co-champion titles at many races, and they continue to train and race today, winning many Master's Division awards.

Training with the best helps one to become the best one can be. It didn't take long for me to realize that I would never again defeat Randy Haas in a race, but daily training as well as sharing ideas and philosophies combined to enable me to run some of the fastest times of my career.

Today, at age forty-nine, Randy Haas continues to win races. His times are a bit slower, and he has been nagged by hamstring problems for the past few years. Still, he laces up the shoes after a double shift, takes his kids to the local track as he grinds out his interval workout, trains early in the morning or after dark, thanks to his demanding work schedule, and refuses to run on the treadmill as much as he refuses to accept failure.

He is the best because he refuses to be anything less.

Joe Muldowney(left), Randy Haas(forefront)
Fort Lauderdale, Florida 1987

MILE 21–TALES FROM THE ROAD

It all happened so quickly.

The gray December sky began to yield snow as we began our training run, a rolling seven-mile course from Pottsville to the small town of Minersville and back.

Rob Crosswell, Brian Tonitis, and I had covered about a mile on the ground that had become slick with a thin layer of snow. We bantered back and forth in a good-natured manner, but, occasionally, barbs were hurled.

Evidently Brian had crossed the line from irreverent to insulting, and Rob reacted. A former high school and collegiate wrestler, his retaliation was swift. In a catlike maneuver, he hurled Tonitis to the snow covered ground, belly first, pinning him. Hooking his forearms under his shoulders, he applied an exaggerated full-nelson, burying his chin deep into the helpless victim's back. Crosswell proceeded to arch Tonitis' spine in a painful, almost medieval torture posture. Arms spread into a three o'clock and a nine o'clock position, Tonitis looked like a crucifixion victim. Indeed, I found out later that the wrestling move is aptly called, 'the crucifix.' Curious drivers, already slowed by the snowy pavement, stared in astonishment at the sight of the two runners, now prone on the slippery street in front of them.

The encounter ended as quickly as it started. Brian lifted his hand in a gesture that signaled 'uncle,' the two combatants then dusted themselves off, and the training run continued. Nothing more was said and the crisis passed.

A few years later, when I felt it was safe to recall the episode to a wounded Tonitis, he proclaimed, "I was sore for three weeks after that incident."

Our running group has trained together for so long that few topics are sacred to us. Sometimes, however, we may catch one another on a bad day and tempers get heated. That day tempers were so hot they practically melted the snow.

An erosion of knee cartilage prematurely ended Rob Crosswell's running career, but not his obsessive fanaticism. Any project on which he embarks is performed over and above the norm.

So, it was no different when he began to rollerblade.

Pottsville, Pennsylvania's terrain is a bit like that of San Francisco. Steep, narrow hills comprise many of the city's streets. Parked cars further constrict the roadways. Harsh northeast winters often leave the streets pock marked with huge craters, and the cinders and road salt, used to melt the winter snow, remain long into the spring until the rains wash them away. Rollerbladers in Santa Monica don't have to deal with such hazards, but Crosswell does.

Rob has had some spectacular collisions with the unforgiving street surface, and he's always emerged bloodied and bruised, but able to complete his workout.

A few years ago, however, one of his crashes put a scare into all of his running companions.

Randy Haas, Mike Dicello, Rob, and I were about a mile from home, at the end of an eight-mile workout. Rob coolly glided on his blades, weaving back and forth on the flat, winding road.

A small stone lodged in one of his wheels, causing it to lock. In what seemed like slow motion, Rob's legs left the ground in front of him, in a double high leg kick, suspending him horizontally. He attempted to break the fall with his hands, but velocity and gravity rendered a full cushioning impossible. His body hit the ground with a thud, and his head snapped back onto the blacktop surface.

We looked back and froze. Turning toward him we attempted to joke, but quickly realized this was far from a joking matter. He lifted his head and uttered intelligible syllables. It sounded like he was speaking in tongues. He tried to get back to his feet but his knees collapsed like a cheap folding chair. He was losing consciousness as we gently lifted him to the side of the road.

I sprinted to a nearby business where I called for an ambulance. I also had the unpleasant task of informing his wife that he presently lay unconscious on the side of a rural road.

The EMTs arrived within minutes, and he was rushed to the emergency room, where he was diagnosed with a concussion. He was held overnight for observation, and was forced to take a few days off.

Within a week he was back on the road, undaunted by his near-death experience, which seemed to affect us more than he.

Not so life-threatening was an experience I encountered fifteen years ago while running with Rob Crosswell.

A popular ten-mile loop course featured two miles on a path that parallels railroad tracks. We were running easily along the tracks, ready to exit for our last two miles home, when my foot nicked the rail. In a cartoon-like attempt to maintain my balance, I crashed to the ground, breaking the fall with my hands.

In an effort to thwart all-terrain vehicles from driving on its property, the railroad company installed large stones, the size of grapefruit, along the path. The heel of my left hand came in contact with one of these rocks as I plummeted to the ground. I cursed, got up, peered at my hand to find a gash, garnished with black silt, oozing blood as well as the contents of the meaty part of my palm. Stung but not disabled, Rob asked if I was ok. I replied in the affirmative and we continued to run. For the next two miles I received more quizzical stares than normal, and it wasn't until I stopped that I realized that I had painted a symmetrical red stripe from my hip to my shoulder, a result of the stream of blood produced from the wound. I rinsed my hand as well as my blood-spattered body, and shoved off to the emergency room. The twelve stitches weren't bad. The scrub brush used to clean the coal silt from the wound was, however, quite unpleasant.

Eric Anchorstar believes that we runners suffer from a distinct lack of respect from others. In addition, his wife is a teacher, a profession that could also use a boost of respect these days. He hears the horror stories of unruly students who often cannot be reprimanded for a myriad of reasons.

On the last mile of his training run his route takes him along a well-traveled street used by middle school students on their way from school. On most days, he endures the whistles, hoots and hollers from the young teens. On occasion, however, he confronts them, informing the verbal offenders, "Your parents or teachers may not be allowed to kick your ass, but I can." Now, he realizes that he can't kick their asses, but so far he's been pretty convincing.

Over the course of my career many local runners have asked if they could train with our group. We'll take on anyone who wants to come along, but we will always inform the newcomers what our pace will be on that given day. Inevitably, though, for some reason, many of those who have joined us on a training run have decided to turn the workout into a race.

One such competition occurred on a winter day back in 1990.

A local runner had requested to train with Randy Haas and me. We told him that we intended to run a hilly, wooded ten-mile course, and that we planned to run a seven-minute per mile pace. Soon after we entered the woods after about two-miles, the race began. Our new partner quickened the pace and we were happy to oblige him. We managed to remain close enough ahead of him to keep him from getting lost, and gained a sizeable lead as we emerged from the woods. By the time we climbed the last mile hill to the finish, Randy and I were four-hundred-yards ahead of him. He was not pleased with the outcome. Despite his desire to push the pace, he complained, "I'd run with you guys again if you were more honest."

Once on an out-and-back ten-mile course, a guest runner sprinted at race pace for the first five miles, the absolute farthest point from the start. Eric Anchorstar and I wondered where this guy came from, as we were always well ahead of him in local races. When I called out our five-mile split, he abruptly stopped! We looked back to see him walking. Apparently, his race ended, he decided to quit. He had a five-mile walk home, and we never trained with him again.

During the two-week whitetail deer season in Pennsylvania most prudent runners take their training to the roads.

Of course, sometimes we are not known for our prudent decisions.

On the final day of the season, back in 1987, Brian and I decided to run one of our favorite courses through Sharp Mountain.

As we topped a large hill, trees stripped bare of their leaves for the coming winter, we rounded a blind curve, past two giant water storage tanks. In front of us, on the path, seventy-five yards ahead, ran a huge buck bearing down toward us. Upon spotting the two colorfully clad figures, he instantly veered right into the thick woods. As we looked ahead, a hundred or so yards ahead, we stared at the barrel of a rifle, sighted in, ready to fire upon the deer.

We never stuck around to observe the hunter's reaction. Instead, we, like the fortunate buck, veered into the woods as well.

During October hunters enjoy bow hunting in the woods of Pennsylvania.

A couple of years ago, I enjoyed a pleasant training run on a magnificent October day. The wooded path was quiet, warm, and bore the odor of freshly dried leaves. As I ran, I was adrift in thought when, suddenly, I thought I heard the voice of God.

"You know that you're on private property." He bellowed.

I looked toward the sky, expecting the heavens to open up. Instead, I saw a camo-clad hunter, bow and arrow in hand. I apologized, turned in the other direction, and never entered his woods again.

Randy Haas turned in one of the best races of his career at the 1991 Philadelphia Distance Run, covering the half marathon course in a time of one hour, 6 minute, and 52 seconds, earning him second place among Americans.

On the way back to the hotel after the race, a group of fellow runners from our area accompanied the local hero. We praised his effort and complimented him on his elite status as the second American finisher. He firmly corrected us, however, informing us that he was, in reality, the first American finisher, as the person who finished ahead of him was actually from New Mexico!

Astonished and waiting for Haas to laugh at the dry joke he played on us, we rapidly realized that his geographic skills lagged far behind his running prowess. He really did think that New Mexico had not yet become part of the United States.

Today, many years later, we still ask Randy to advise us on geographic matters.

For the past five years I have coached cross country at our Penn State Schuylkill Campus, a satellite campus of Penn State University. Each year much of my team consists of inner city youth, many of whom are African American, and many of whom receive quite a culture shock upon entering the rural world of northeastern Pennsylvania.

I enjoy running with the team, taking them on the shaded roads and trails that are ideal running venues for cross country runners.

Often, of course, these trails bring us in close contact with nature.

Two years ago, six team members and I were running an easy four-miler the day before a race. Five of the team members were African American. On a secluded path we were confronted by a snarling dog, which waited until the last runner passed before giving chase. The last runner, Dante, escaped the snarling animal, and when we reached safety exclaimed, "Coach, I don't think that dog likes black folks!" We all laughed, and I replied, "Dante, look around.... I think he just didn't like you."

It doesn't take too long for runners to fill the vault with road tales. Daily training becomes like a moving theatrical production, complete with a cast, an audience and a stage. It becomes part of what defines us, what makes us different from other people in other sports. It is a continuing drama with a script that is revised each time we begin our workout.

FINISH LINE

I feel a sense of guilt.

This book is a compilation of my thoughts, feelings, 'expert' advice, and fond recollections of my life as a long distance runner.

The entire process of writing and researching for this book was way too much fun.

But, then, that term appropriately sums up my life as a runner. It has been way too much fun.

My daily training has, figuratively, taken me around the world approximately four times. Along the way I have accumulated worlds of experiences, met some fascinating individuals, made lifelong friendships, and felt the exhilaration of success as well as the sting of disappointment.

To me, running and racing reflects my philosophy of life. I believe it is the philosophy that built America, and distinguishes us as Americans. I also believe, in some ways, it is a diminishing American ethic today. It is the philosophy of rugged individualism.

I am empowered by the fact that when I train and race, I control my own running destiny. I have no one else but me to blame for my failure or to credit for my success. There are no excuses. I accept my fate because I'm the one who controls that fate. If I can help others to become better runners, if I can impart what I've learned to others, I feel as though I've given back.

Too often today, folks point to others for their shortcomings.

Consider the term, "Overserved."

"I was overserved last night."

No, you CHOSE to drink too much. 'Overserved' implies that someone else caused you to consume too much. Self discipline and self control are personal responsibilities. Don't get me wrong, we all veer off the path of self control in our lives, but, more often than not, we only have ourselves to blame.

My fondest wish is that you, as a runner, enjoy your journey as much as I have enjoyed mine.

We participate in this sport for a variety of reasons, but our experiences are the same. When I encounter runners who are new to the sport I am renewed by their enthusiasm, their goal-setting, and their anticipation about what is on the horizon for them in their running career.

This book was written for both the new runners and the old.

Whether you've recently begun your journey or if your best miles are behind you I hope you encounter more downhills than uphills. I hope your days are sunny and pleasant. I hope you continue to achieve personal bests, but most of all I hope your journey is long, rich, and filled with happiness and success.

I'll see you on the road.

Joe

BIBLIOGRAPHY

Several sources were researched in order to obtain some of the factual information contained in this book. I gratefully acknowledge the following works.

Brown Budoff, Carrie. (1 April 2008). "Extreme Makeover: Pennsylvania Edition". *Politico*.

Buford, Kate. *Native American Son: The Life and Sporting Legend of Jim Thorpe* Knopf, 2010.

Cooper, Kenneth. *Aerobics.* New York: M. Evans, distributed in association with Lippincott, Philadelphia, 1968.

Epstein, David (5 August 2008). "Catching Up With Frank Shorter". *Sports Illustrated.*

http://www.absoluteastronomy.com/topics/Pottsville,_Pennsylvania January 14, 2011.

http://www.baa.org/About/BAA-History.aspx. Retreived 13 February 2011.

http://republicanherald.com/sports/u-s-in-another-running-boom-1.469153. Republican HeraldDecember 8, 2009.

Karon, Tony (12 September 2000). "Revisiting the Olympics' Darkest Day". *Time.*

Moore, Kenny. *Bowerman and the Men of Oregon.* Emmaus, Pennsylvania: Rodale Press, 2006.

Moore, Kenny (18 September 1972). "Shootings in the Night". *Sports Illustrated.*

Thorpe's son seeks return of remains, Associated Press, 25 June 2011.

Wheeler, Robert W. *Jim Thorpe, World's Greatest Athlete*, University of Oklahoma Press. 1979.